MANAGING
ORGANIZATIONAL INNOVATION

The Irwin-Dorsey Series in Behavioral Science

MANAGING

ORGANIZATIONAL

INNOVATION

JEREMIAH J. O'CONNELL
Wharton School of Finance and Commerce
University of Pennsylvania

1968
RICHARD D. IRWIN, INC.
Homewood, Illinois

First Printing, January, 1968

Library of Congress Catalog Card No. 67–23769
PRINTED IN THE UNITED STATES OF AMERICA

To Pat

PREFACE

Reality. *In our endeavor to understand reality, we are somewhat like a man trying to understand the mechanism of a closed watch. He sees the face and the moving hands, even hears its ticking, but he has no way of opening the case.*

If he is ingenious, he may form some picture of a mechanism for all the things that he observed, but he may never be sure that his picture is the only one which could explain his observations. He will never be able to compare his picture with the mechanism and he cannot even imagine the possibility and meaning of such comparison.—EINSTEIN

If physical reality relented so begrudgingly to the inquiry of the genius Einstein, how humble must the researcher be who attempts to understand the reality of a complex human organization! How careful, too, must the reader be in accepting the author's picture of reality! To say *caveat lector* is not sufficient. The author urges the reader to join him in the inquiry. If the author can be accepted as a reliable witness, the reader will find the data in this book to form his own picture of reality. Chapters three, four, five, and six record the author's observations of a management consultant assisting an insurance company in a major reorganization effort. On the basis of this description, the reader is invited to challenge the explanations and evaluations offered by the author in the final three chapters. Because the story gets rather involved, a capsule version here may help keep the facts in perspective.

Top management of a giant life insurance company sought the aid of a management consulting firm in solving a "problem" in its several hundred branch offices. Expenses were climbing, and the rate of premium growth was lagging. The "heat was on" to improve performance. The consultant's diagnosis showed a need for a new marketing strategy to place the best resources in the most promising markets. Crucial to this end was the provision of more personal supervision of the thousands of agents. This meant inserting a line management level between each branch manager and his two dozen or more agents, one first-line supervisor to about each seven agents. The new first-line supervisor became the hub of a new planning and control system designed in the spirit of management by objectives.

This study puts the spotlight on the first-line supervisor as the key to change in the insurance company. The consultant had to design a way to make effective line managers out of men who had previously filled staff positions in each branch office. The critical inquiry in the chapters that follow focuses on the manner in which the consultant filled his change agent role in managing this organizational innovation.

The author will be forgiven, he trusts, if for the sake of clarity he sometimes oversimplifies a point of theory or if for the sake of emphasis he polarizes positions. George Homans may be right when he says that the problem of this field is that too many people get impaled on the horns of false dichotomies. Not wishing to contribute to such delinquency, the author reminds the reader: "The map is not the territory!"

In the chain of events which led to the unique opportunity to do the research for this book two people stand out. Professor Robert H. Guest of the Amos Tuck School of Business Administration sparked interest in the field of organizational change. Mr. Douglas Williams of Douglas Williams Associates patiently listened to and sagely commented on early formulations of this research design. Professors Melvin Anshen, John G. Hutchinson, Matthew B. Miles, Robert H. Guest, and especially Charles E. Summer provided helpful critique in the early stages of the manuscript. A special word of appreciation must go to Professor Warren G. Bennis who in his own writings and in his specific comments on this manuscript aided in clarifying the author's own thoughts. The author acknowledges with appreciation the assistance provided by the Wharton School of Finance and Commerce in preparing this study for publication.

Those who have contributed most to this study must remain unnamed. Both insurance company and consulting firm deserve praise for not only allowing but welcoming this unprecedented study. The author was granted absolutely free access by both parties, and both parties scrupulously honored the author's independence. The author cannot pay higher tribute to client and consultant than to say he could not desire more in his relationship with them than was given him.

December, 1967   JEREMIAH J. O'CONNELL

TABLE OF CONTENTS

CHAPTER ONE

Toward a Theory of Organizational Change

INTRODUCTION

ONE OF THE AREAS within the field of organization theory receiving increasing attention is the area of organizational change. Theorists are attempting to understand and reduce to model form the process of change in complex organizations. For the most part, the theorists rely on empirical data from the efforts of academic practitioners to apply particular techniques in producing organizational change. A second type of practitioner—the professional management consultant—uses a more pragmatically eclectic approach in assisting clients to produce organizational change. The increased interest in this area is reflected in the recent literature, especially in the past few years. No single factor explains this surge of interest. Psychologists, social psychologists, and sociologists laid the theoretical foundation some years ago, beginning with developments in knowledge about the dynamics of change in individuals (learning models, attitude change models, and others) and moving to improved knowledge about group dynamics. An eagerness among some social scientists not only to understand human phenomena but to influence human affairs moved some of these practitioners more deeply into the area of organizational change. At the same time, administrators of organizations, particularly of business organizations, were becoming increasingly ready to accept help in guiding their organizations through change. Various pressures seemed to be mounting that required adjustments in the programmed sets of behavior patterns that make up organizations. Accelerated technological change was

1

putting new and heavy demands on the organization. Specifically, the emerging technology and techniques of the "systems approach" seemed to presage a shift in emphasis from the economics of specialization and economies of scale to the economics of coordination. The central thrust in the search for organizational efficiency would come from coordinative efforts more than from finer division of labor and size-induced economies. The quest for economies through coordination often required quite radical and extensive organizational change. In such an environment the social-science practitioner found opportunity to apply his theoretical knowledge, and the management consultant found increased demand for his experienced skill.

Obviously it is too early for a general theory of organizational change. The social scientists involved can have faced only a narrow range of situations in application of their somewhat restricted techniques. Only very recently have participant-observer and nonparticipant-observer studies of such projects appeared in the literature. It will be some time yet before social scientists not directly involved will have data rich and complete enough on which to base a general theory. While social-science practitioner and management-consultant practitioner have just recently begun some formal dialogue in search of mutual enlightenment, to the researcher's knowledge, no careful study exists in the literature of the professional management consultant at work assisting a client in organizational change. This gap in the literature—in large measure explained by the consultant's professional and commercial responsibility to his clients—stands in the way of theoretical development of the field of organizational change. The persons having the most experience with organizational change have not enriched the literature with their experiences nor have direct observers been present to record such data. Only when the empirical record shows a range of studies of many kinds of change agents at work in many different situations will theorizing be well founded. We are a long way from being able to give sound answers to such questions as the following: Is there one best way to manage organizational change in complex business enterprises? Is there a trustworthy formula for planning and controlling shifts in the programmed sets of behavior patterns that make up organizations? What roles are appropriate for the change agent under what kinds of circumstances? What focus or value orientation should guide the change agent in coping with the technological, structural, and social factors in organizations? What techniques or intervention strategies will work best for the change agent under what conditions? What is the best way to control planned organizational change?

The research reported here is meant to bring us a little closer to being able to answer these questions about organizational change. Its significance derives from the fact that this study fits into the gap in the literature mentioned above, that is, the lack of documentation of the professional management consultant acting in the change agent role.

PROGRESS TO DATE IN UNDERSTANDING ORGANIZATIONAL CHANGE

To place this research in context, it is necessary briefly to point out from the literature some of the landmark contributions made to the understanding of organizational change. The references used here of necessity must be indicative rather than exhaustive of the richness and complexity of the conceptual underpinnings of the field of organization change.[1] Of course, dependency should be admitted on virtually the whole spectrum of advances in the social sciences dealing with the dynamics of human affairs on three levels: (1) within the individual as a system, (2) in two-person systems, and (3) in multiple person, nonhierarchical systems. Advances here set the stage for progress in organizational change, that is, change in hierarchical systems. On the first level, psychologists progressed beyond static models of man to dynamic models of the human organism perceiving, being motivated, learning, and maturing. While all these conceptual building blocks provide the necessary foundation for progress on the other levels, the models of the maturing personality developed by such men as Abraham Maslow, Gordon Allport, and Carl Rogers[2] have been the stepping-off point for most of the inquiry and involvement of social scientists in the particular

---

[1]To date no one has attempted a thorough study of the historical development of this aspect of social science nor is there even a relatively complete, annotated bibliography of the relevant literature. A helpful review of part of the literature appears as an appendix in Guest, Robert H., *Organizational Change: The Effect of Successful Leadership* (Homewood, Ill.: Richard D. Irwin, Inc., and The Dorsey Press, 1962). One other fine though incomplete source is *The Planning of Change*, eds. Bennis, Warren G., Benne, Kenneth D., and Chin, Robert (New York: Holt, Rinehart & Winston, 1962). The Foundation for Research on Human Behavior is now in the process of developing what promises to be a comprehensive bibliography.

[2]Maslow, Abraham H., *Motivation and Personality* (New York: Harper & Row, 1954); Allport, Gordon W., *Personality and Social Encounter* (Boston: Beacon Press, 1960); Rogers, Carl R., *On Becoming a Person* (Cambridge, Mass.: Riverside Press, 1961).

field of organizational change. Certainly, on the level of the two-person system, the helping professions of clinical psychology and psychiatry have made substantial progress in theory development on the process of individual personality change through counseling or psychotherapy. Representative, and in the mainstream again, would be the work of Carl Rogers.[3] On the third level, the involvement of change agents with nonhierarchical groups has received much attention in both experimental and case studies. A reference or two will indicate the range of the work done on this level.

Otto Pollak has done much with social-work efforts in family therapy.[4] It was natural that some of the group dynamics activity, sparked in part by the Western Electric Studies of the late 1920's and early 1930's, was devoted to learning more about inducing behavioral changes in groups. Some of the most relevant group dynamics experiments grew out of Kurt Lewin's concept of group behavior as processes in quasi-stationary equilibrium.[5] Lewin himself experimented with groups of housewives in changing food usage habits.[6] Working with more structured groups, Coch and French conducted similar experiments,[7] as did Levine and Butler.[8] Certainly, with admitted dependency on Lewin's theories, the early post-World War II work in laboratory training at Bethel, Maine, significantly affected the whole field of behavioral change.[9] Sensitivity training developed as an approach to behavioral change in nonhierarchical groups initially and only later, in 1958, found application in formal,

---

[3]Rogers, Carl R., and Dymond, R. F., *Psychotherapy and Personality Change* (Chicago: University of Chicago Press, 1957) ; Rogers, Carl R., "A Process Conception of Psychotherapy," *The American Psychologist,* XIII (No. 4, April 1958) , 142–49.

[4]Pollak, Otto, "Entrance of the Caseworker into Family Interaction," *Social Casework* (April 1964) , and "Worker Assignment in Casework with Marriage Partners," *The Social Service Review,* XXXVII (No. 1, March 1963) , 41–53, and "Issues in Family Diagnosis and Family Therapy," *Journal of Marriage and the Family,* XXVI (No. 3, 1964) , 279–87.

[5]Lewin, Kurt, "Studies in Group Decision," in *Group Dynamics: Research and Theory,* eds. Cartwright, D., and Zander, A. (Evanston, Ill.: Row, Peterson & Co., 1953) .

[6]Lewin, Kurt, "Group Decisions and Social Change" in *Readings in Social Psychology,* eds. Maccoby, E. E., Hartley, E. L., and Newcomb, T. M. (New York: Holt, Rinehart & Winston, 1958) .

[7]Coch, Lester, and French, John R. P., Jr., "Overcoming Resistance to Change," *Human Relations,* I (No. 4, 1948) , 512–32.

[8]Levine, Jacob, and Butler, John, "Lecture vs. Group Decision in Changing Behavior," *Journal of Applied Psychology,* XXXVI (1952) , 29–33.

[9]For an historical perspective see National Training Laboratory in Group Development, *Explorations in Human Relations: An Assessment of Experience 1947–1953* (Washington, D.C., 1953) . More recent developments are rather well recorded in the *Journal of Applied Behavioral Science.*

hierarchical, organizations with the initiation of the organization improvement efforts at ESSO.[10]

Without such prior inquiry into the dynamics of individual and group behavior the relatively recent work on change in hierarchical systems could not have been so productive. It is important to note, too, that because of the character of the prior research and because of the people involved, most social scientists currently working on organizational change seem to have converged on a narrow range of approaches. This is true, at least as the recent literature reflects the kinds of organizational change activities in progress. Attention is drawn toward the types of organization change efforts undertaken by Shepard and Blake at ESSO[11] or by "a Swiss industrial social psychologist" in "an international Swiss firm"[12] or by Blake and Mouton in "Sigma" company[13] or by Argyris with the boards of two research organizations.[14] Applications of sensitivity training and the "managerial grid" command much of the attention of those involved in organizational change. This is not to deny that other approaches are being used and reported in the literature—for example, Mann's use of the survey feedback method for effecting organizational change or Whyte's action research in the Tremont Hotel.[15] Some of the earlier and now-classic case studies of organizational change (where no outside change agent was involved) do not show this same preoccupation with special techniques to effect the change.[16] The point remains that the current central thrust in social-science investigation of organizational change comes from a rather narrowly defined segment of the social-science fraternity.

[10]The Foundation for Research on Human Behavior, *An Action Research Program for Organization Improvement* (Ann Arbor, Mich., 1960) .

[11]*Ibid.*

[12]Bennis, Warren G., *Bureaucracy and Social Change: Anatomy of a Failure* (Cambridge, Mass.: The M.I.T. Press, 1963) .

[13]Blake, Robert R., Mouton, Jane S., Barnes, Louis B., and Greiner, Larry E., "Breakthrough in Organizational Development," *Harvard Business Review* (November-December 1964) , 133–46.

[14]Argyris, Chris, "Creating and Evaluating Organizational Change," paper presented at Foundation for Research on Human Behavior conference at the Onchiota Conference Center, Tuxedo, New York, July 13, 1965.

[15]Mann, Floyd C., "Studying and Creating Change: A Means to Understanding Social Organization," in *Research in Industrial Human Relations* (No. 17, 1957) , 146–67; Whyte, William Foote, and Hamilton, Edith Lentz, *Action Research for Management* (Homewood, Ill.: Richard D. Irwin, Inc., and the Dorsey Press, 1964) .

[16]See, e.g., Blau, Peter, *The Dynamics of Bureaucracy* (Chicago: University of Chicago Press, 1955) ; Gouldner, Alvin W., *Patterns of Industrial Bureaucracy* (New York: The Free Press, 1954) ; Lawrence, Paul R., *The Changing of Organizational Behavior Patterns* (Cambridge, Mass.: Harvard University Press, 1958) ; Guest, *op. cit.*

The character of this recent effort can best be appreciated by an inquiry into, first, the role identified as appropriate for the change agent as he attempts to help a client system; second, the focus or value orientation of the change agent; and third, the intervention strategies utilized by the change agent.

No standard terminology has yet been developed for the various change-agent roles in this relatively new area of organizational change. Warren Bennis speaks of "researchers, trainers, consultants, teachers, and counselors" in his article on the subject.[17] Bennis sees the change agent wearing two or more of these hats in any one engagement, probably in a particular sequence with more emphasis on one than the others. Our purposes here will be served by a simpler set of categories describing the range of change agent roles. The modal role performance of change agents reported in the literature may be seen as falling somewhere along a collaborative-unilateral continuum. The available descriptions of change agent behavior tend to fall more toward the collaborative end of the scale.[18]

Warren Bennis is a good witness for the evolving focus or value orientation of many of those currently involved in organizational change: "There is growing disenchantment with the moral neutrality of the scientist. . . . For social scientists and actionists, for example, the infusion of democratic values in bureaucratic institutions remains an unconquered promise."[19]

Not only have some social scientists abandoned moral neutrality in their change-agent roles, but some appear to have become crusaders for democratic values.[20] Borrowing from the terminology used in the operations research technique of linear programming, we might say the focus adopted by these social scientists tends to maximize human values within the constraints of economic values—in contrast to scientific management's alleged tendency to maximize economic values within the constraints of human values. This focus or value orientation leads these social scientists to emphasize the

---

[17]Bennis, Warren G., "A New Role for the Behavioral Sciences: Effecting Organizational Change," *Administrative Science Quarterly* (September 1963) , 142.

[18]The oversimplification here in role definition must be viewed in the context of our separate treatment of role, focus, and intervention strategies of the change agent. Others have subsumed all three aspects under the one label "role."

[19]Bennis, *op. cit.*, pp. 128–29.

[20]See, for instance, Benne, Kenneth D., "Democratic Ethics and Human Engineering," in Bennis *et al.*, *op. cit.* Note how consistent this theme is in this volume, particularly in Part One, pp. 7–186. Bennis treats this topic quite fully in his *Changing Organizations* (New York: McGraw-Hill Book Company, 1966) .

social aspect of organizations and to seek leverage for organizational change not in structural or technical factors but in social or interpersonal factors.[21]

The intervention strategies currently so much in use by such social scientists as Argyris, Blake, Bennis, Shepard, Miles, Schein, and others quite naturally fit the collaborative change-agent role and the human values focus. The strategies draw group members in as architects, engineers, and fabricators of whatever change is to take place. Sensitivity or laboratory training would be the least structured participative device,[22] while the managerial grid technique[23] includes more substantive inputs from the change agent. These, especially, represent the strategy Sayles has in mind when he speaks of the "conversion approach,"[24] where changed organizational behavior is the product of individual cognitive or attitudinal change. Similar intervention strategies in which the change agent was more active in varying degrees would be Floyd Mann's survey feedback techniques[25] and William F. Whyte's action research[26] where either attitude survey data and/or social-science theory are infused into the client system in an effort to induce change. Also, under the umbrella-type rubric of "action research" other maieutic intervention strategies are used. In an insurance company, for example, the consultants told the client:

An important assumption underlying the proposed study is that with proper guidance and leadership the organization itself is capable of developing its own ideas for self-improvement. The role of the consultant is to bring these ideas into focus, to reflect them back to management, and to discuss courses of action which are internally consistent and, at the same time, which are consistent with the latest and most effective administrative practices in business. The project to be undertaken is to be viewed as a cooperative effort and not one in which the consultant attempts to "sell" specific pro-

---

[21]Harold J. Leavitt discusses these three points of leverage in "Applied Organizational Change in Industry: Structural, Technological, and Humanistic Approaches," in *New Perspectives in Organization Research*, eds. Cooper, W. W., Leavitt, H. J., and Shelley, M. (New York: John Wiley & Sons, Inc., 1964).

[22]See especially Argyris, Chris, *Interpersonal Competence and Organizational Effectiveness* (Homewood, Ill.: Richard D. Irwin, Inc., and The Dorsey Press, 1962); also Foundation for Research on Human Behavior, *An Action Research Program for Organization Improvement* (Ann Arbor, Michigan, 1960).

[23]Blake *et al.*, *op. cit.*

[24]Sayles, Leonard R., "The Change Process in Organizations: An Applied Anthropology Analysis," *Human Organization*, XXI (No. 2, Summer 1962), 66.

[25]Mann, *op. cit.*

[26]Whyte and Hamilton, *op. cit.*

grams or systems. The value of the project lies in helping management discover its *own* strengths and abilities and to maximize the potential which already exists.[27]

In the Leeds engagement the consultants themselves were catalysts, and their diagnostic report (an ordered synthesis of interview data) became a catalyst when all supervisory levels of the organization examined it in feedback sessions. No recommendations were given by the consultants. Change efforts began at all levels and on many different issues, however, and the consultants nondirectively assisted top management in setting priorities, in giving direction to the grass roots change efforts, and in coordinating the change efforts at all levels in the organization. A similar type of intervention strategy is employed by Robert H. Schaffer and Associates in their consulting practice.

The principal objective of our firm is to develop workable methods for helping large, complex organizations increase their effectiveness by:

1. Making significantly greater use of the capacities, talents and energies available to them, and, in consequence,

2. Providing the increased rewards and gratifications which result from work that is more demanding, more engaging, more meaningful.

Two operational features distinguish our practice from more traditional management consulting or management engineering:

1. Each of our assignments is, in effect, action research undertaken in collaboration with the client. The work is always defined in terms of accomplishing specific, measurable improvements. We do not undertake assignments whose chief purpose is diagnostic, nor do we produce reports with lists of recommendations about what management *ought* to do.

2. The traditional consultant's value is based on knowledge and skill that permit him to fill a void in the organization's resources. Our value lies in helping management discover the organization's own latent strengths and abilities, and in helping them learn how to put this capacity to work.[28]

Most recent social-science involvement, then, in organizational

———————
[27]From the proposal for a consulting engagement at the Leeds Insurance Company, conducted by Dr. Robert H. Guest with the collaboration of this researcher.

[28]From the brochure explaining the services offered by Robert H. Schaffer and Associates.

change has tended to have the following characteristics: (1) change-agent role is more collaborative than unilateral, (2) a human values focus causes emphasis on the social more than the structural or technological factors in organization, and (3) intervention strategies aim at behavioral change through cognitive or attitude change rather than through a direct alteration of the external forces which constitute the role demands. Such is the manner in which these social science practitioners would respond to the questions posed in the introduction of this chapter about the planning of organizational change. As change agents, they plan organizational change, using as planning premises the above conceptions of role, focus, and intervention strategy. Hence, social-science progress in building a theory of planned change in hierarchical systems is moving down a rather narrow path.

Happily the social scientists involved in organizational change programs often meticulously describe their efforts in books and journal articles. Especially important to the development of organization change theory are the evaluation studies of such organizational changes. Some evaluations have been performed by participants in the change programs.[29] Particularly promising are evaluations of nonparticipants[30] and the increasingly more ambitious research designs being employed in these evaluations.[31] These studies are providing a sounder basis for the development of the whole field of organizational change theory.

[29]See, for instance, Shepard's work reported in Foundation for Research on Human Behavior, *op. cit.*, Argyris, *op. cit.*, and Blake, Robert R., and Mouton, Jane S., "Some Effects of Managerial Grid Seminar Training on Union and Management Attitudes Toward Supervision," *The Journal of Applied Behavioral Science*, Vol. 2, No. 4, 1966, 387–400.

[30]Blake, Robert R., Mouton, Jane S., Barnes, Louis B., and Greiner, Larry E., "Breakthrough in Organizational Development," *Harvard Business Review*, November-December 1964, 133–55.

[31]Greiner, Larry, "Research on the Managerial Grid Approach to Organizational Development," paper presented at the Foundation for Research on Human Behavior conference at the Onchiota Conference Center, Tuxedo, New York, July 12, 1965; Miles, Matthew B., "Methodological Problems in Evaluating Organizational Change: Two Illustrations," paper presented at the Foundation for Research on Human Behavior conference at the Onchiota Conference Center, Tuxedo, New York, July 13, 1965; Miles, Matthew B., "Learning Processes and Outcomes in Human Relations Training," in *Personal and Organizational Change Through Group Methods* by Schein, Edgar E., and Bennis, Warren G. (New York: John Wiley & Sons, Inc., 1965), 244–54; Bunker, Douglas R., "Individual Applications of Laboratory Training," *The Journal of Applied Behavioral Science*, Vol. 1, No. 2, 1965, 131–48; Valiquet, M. I., "Contribution to the Evaluation of a Management Training Program," unpublished doctoral dissertation, Massachusetts Institute of Technology, 1964.

WHERE THIS RESEARCH FITS AND ITS CONTRIBUTION

Full development of theory about planned organization change must await more systematic inquiry into change efforts planned without the narrowing constraints of the planning premises about role, focus, and intervention strategy adopted by most social-science practitioners currently active in the field. This research is one effort to fill this gap in the literature. It reports about a change agent who adopts an "unilateral" role, who focuses particularly on economic rather than human values in engineering the structural factors rather than social factors in organizations, and who uses intervention strategies that reshape the external forces which constitute role demands rather than change the people directly. This change agent's relative success in attaining the goals of the planned change raises the question of whether there is one best way to plan organizational change, as some social scientists would suggest. This research challenges the position that the planning premises of role, focus, and intervention strategy should be predetermined as if by some value imperative. Given the multiple, and sometimes conflicting, objectives of business enterprises and the wide range of the kinds of organizational change needs, should not the change agent choose his role, focus, and intervention strategies on the basis of a prudential judgment of the facts of the situation, the conditions existing when he enters the client system? This research points to just such a relationship between entry conditions and the planning premises. Also, this research, in the sense that it is an evaluation of a planned change effort, goes a step beyond what has been done to date. The evaluations that appear in the literature use case study, attitude survey, or experimentation to answer the question: "How effective has the planned change program been?" There has been little practical recognition of organizational change as a process. Most evaluations treat change as an event. Further, the evaluations have been academic exercises largely for the edification of the social scientist practitioner. This research wrestles more with the question: "How effective is the planned change program during the transition from 'before' to 'after'?" An attempt is made to construct a model for the continual evaluation of the change program in process. This approach recognizes the manager's need to know "how things are going" while the change is in transition so that he can take appropriate corrective action if and when it is needed. By so broadening the concept of evaluation to include the familiar management concept of control, it becames dramatically evident that "control" data must be a synthesis of behavior data and economic performance data.

In summary, then, this research offers the first systematic, non-participant, observer study of a professional management consultant in his change-agent role. The management consulting industry is fast approaching the billion-dollar mark in annual billings and, hence, has to be considered a significant force in change, including organizational change, in American industry. Yet, theoretical development of the field of organization change has been progressing as if the management consultant had nothing to offer. This research begins to show how much is to be learned by drawing on the management consultant's experience in the search for models of organization change.

CHAPTER TWO

Research Design

INTRODUCTION

THIS STUDY is a nonparticipant observer's record of an engagement between one of the world's largest management consulting firms and one of the world's largest insurance companies. A worsening competitive position made the company aware of the need for change. With the help of the consultant, the client executives recognized the need for organizational change rather than for a change in product, price, promotion, technology, personnel, or the like. Simply stated, in order to significantly increase premium income at less expense, the company had to position the best resources possible in the most promising markets. In classical management terms, this entailed the installation of a radically new, decentralized planning and control system. Essentially, people in the four supervisory levels below the senior vice president of the Personal Life Sales Division had to behave quite differently toward both their superiors and subordinates. While change at every level was critical, all effort would be in vain unless the first-line supervisor, who had direct contact with the agents generating the dollars of premium income, could be made to behave in a new way. Only when the three or four first-line supervisors in each of the several hundred branch offices adopted a new behavior pattern could the company feel confident that the best resources would be positioned and maintained in the most promising markets. This research records the consultant's efforts to manage the first-line supervisor's change from a staff person to a fully responsible line manager. This clinical material yields some insights

13

into how one of the most practiced management consulting firms views its change-agent role and what techniques it uses when faced with organizational change of mammoth proportions and enormous consequences. The consultant's relative success prompts some conceptualizing—technically, hypotheses based on a singular case study —about the planning and control of organizational change.

RESEARCH OBJECTIVES

Stated specifically, the objectives in this research are threefold. First, the researcher wishes to add to the empirical foundation for the development of the field of organization change. Clinical case studies are a necessary preliminary step in scientific progress in this area. This case study is intended to begin to fill the gap in the literature—cases reporting the work of directive change agents. (The case study will appear in Chapters Three through Six.) Second, based on the case description, the researcher intends to explain why the consultant achieved the degree of success he did in changing the behavior of the insurance company's first-line supervisors from staff to line managers. After examining the appropriateness of the planning premises, the researcher will indicate how major phases of the consultant's plans for effecting the change contributed to the relative success of the change program. The researcher will then explain the causes for the major deviations from the consultant's change program. After this analytic treatment of the clinical data about the behavioral change of the insurance company's first-line supervisors, the researcher will conceptualize some more general conclusions about the planning of changes in organizational behavior in any company. (These specific and general conclusions about the planning of change will appear in Chapter Seven.) Third, the researcher intends to propose a model that will satisfy the practical requirements for controlling the first-line supervisor's behavior change during transition. That is, a model will be presented showing (1) the kinds of data about first-line supervisor behavior and performance necessary for transitional control and (2) the technique for using these data in a logical diagnosis prior to the taking of appropriate corrective action. Finally, this model will be examined for its general applicability to the controlling of the process of planned organization change. (These conclusions about the controlling of change appear in Chapter Eight.)

RESEARCH DESIGN

The dependent variable in this clinical case study is the behavior of the first-line supervisor in the insurance company branch sales office. In Chapter Three, first-line supervisor behavior is described as it was prior to the change. Chapter Four specifies the basic influences—determinants or constraints—of the first-line supervisor behavior described in Chapter Three.

The study concentrates on the consultant's strategies and planned manipulations of the basic influences on first-line supervisor behavior as independent variables (see Chapter Five) . The results of the consultant's efforts to change the first-line supervisor from a staff to a line manager appear in Chapter Six.[1] The case study can be viewed as moving through four stages: (1) description of preconversion[2] behavior and the influences molding it; (2) indentification of the behavior proposed by the consultant and of the strategies and plans designed to produce it; (3) presentation of the postconversion behavior of the first-line supervisor; (4) analysis of (3) in light of (1) and (2) .

METHODS AND DATA

This is a clinical case study based on observation and interviews, supplemented by data from the secondary sources of consultant re-

---

[1]The first-line supervisor position upon which this case focuses bears different titles before and after the change. The "before" title is used in Chapters Three and Four. The "after" title is used in Chapters Five through Eight (see the capitalized titles in the branch office "before and after" organizations pictured below) .

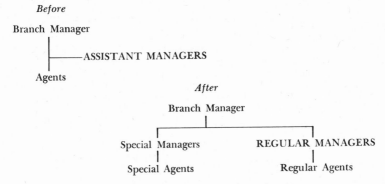

Before

Branch Manager

—————ASSISTANT MANAGERS

Agents

After

Branch Manager

Special Managers   REGULAR MANAGERS

Special Agents   Regular Agents

[2]The consultant used "conversion" to mean the formal introduction of the consulting recommendations in a branch. The title "Line Management" was applied to the recommendations as a whole.

ports and company records. The researcher basically relies on personally conducted "before" and "after" research in two offices, hereafter referred to as offices 7 and 8 (four first-line supervisors). The "before" data in Chapter Three are enriched from consultant reports, especially concerning offices 1 through 6, and from company records. Personally conducted research in offices 1 through 6 (18 first-line supervisors), consultant reports, and company records supplement the "after" data in Chapter Six. All the data on first-line supervisor behavior, except the "before" data from offices 1 through 6, were gathered firsthand by this researcher.

Observation and interviews in offices 7 and 8 took almost eight weeks in the six-month period—beginning one month prior to conversion.

Offices 1 through 6 had the most past experience under Line Management at the time of the research field work—five of the six had almost a year and a half, and the sixth had almost a year. Visits to these offices took five weeks. In all, the field work in the eight offices and the research in the home offices of client and consultant occupied six out of the nine months between November 1963 and July 1964.

All the respondents understood the author's role to be an academic researcher completely independent from both the insurance company and the consultant. Assurances of anonymity based on this independent role were very well received, largely because the role set up a relationship unique in the experience of these particular respondents.

Observation and interview data were openly written while observing and interviewing. As soon after the event as the researcher could find privacy, a taped record was made from these penciled notes for later transcription.

Preconversion and postconversion first-line supervisor behavior makes up the core of the research data. Validity and reliability are best served by adopting the descriptive categories used in data gathering and analysis of organizational behavior by Professors Paul R. Lawrence[3] and Robert H. Guest[4] in recent studies. These authors

---

[3]Lawrence, Paul R., *The Changing of Organizational Behavior Patterns* (Cambridge, Mass.: Harvard University Press, 1958).

[4]Guest, Robert H., *Organizational Change: The Effect of Successful Leadership* (Homewood, Ill.: Richard D. Irwin, Inc., and the Dorsey Press, 1962).

represent a tradition of anthropologists and sociologists[5] who categorize the elements of behavior without rising higher on the level of abstraction than activities, interactions, and sentiments. These or similar terms are used in the tradition either as descriptive categories, as rubrics in data-gathering methodologies, or as essential concepts in a theory. The researcher's debt to this tradition is for a model that validly describes human behavior. The terms "activities," "interactions," and "sentiments" are used in this study to give structure to observation and data gathering and to assure the maximum amount of uniformity of categories so necessary in before-and-after studies. The researcher has used the classification categories of the interactionists without reference to their powerful predictive theories about the relationships among activities, interactions, and sentiments. In this, the researcher follows the lead of both Guest and Lawrence. Since the mission in this case study is to throw clinical light on the change process and to generate some first-level generalizations about planning and controlling change, the dependent and independent variables are defined differently than in Homans' work, for instance. Here, the activities, interactions, and sentiments taken as a whole, which describe first-line supervisor behavior, constitute the dependent variable. The consultant's plans are the independent variables. It is the causal relationship between these independent and dependent variables that must be analyzed to meet this study's objectives, not the causal relationships among the activities, interactions, and sentiments that define first-line supervisor behavior. However, by selecting these descriptive categories, the researcher recognizes the implicit acceptance of the validity of the interactionists' predictive theories. Indeed, the assumption about the causal relationships among activities, interactions, and sentiments becomes explicit in many places in this study.

---

[5]The major phases in this tradition are found in the following: Chapple, Eliot D., and Coon, Carleton, *Principles of Anthropology* (New York: Holt, Rinehart & Winston, 1942) ; Homans, George C., *The Human Group* (New York: Harcourt, Brace & World, 1950) ; Whyte, William F., "Framework for the Analysis of Industrial Relations," *Industrial and Labor Relations Review,* III (No. 3, April 1950) , 393–401; Arensberg, Conrad M., "Behavior and Organization: Industrial Studies," *Social Psychology at the Crossroads,* eds. Rohrer, John J., and Sherif, Muzafer (New York: Harper & Row, 1951) ; Chapple, Eliot D., and Sayles, Leonard R., *The Measure of Management* (New York: The Macmillan Co., 1961) ; Whyte, William Foote, and Hamilton, Edith Lentz, *Action Research for Management* (Homewood, Ill.: Richard D. Irwin, Inc., and the Dorsey Press, 1964) .

Due to some shading of definitions of these categories within the tradition itself, and also due to constraints on the type of observation possible under the circumstances of this study, it will be necessary to define the categories. "Activities" shall mean objectively observable physical action,[6] expressed not in the lowest level of abstraction —for example, writing, walking, talking—but in the next higher level of abstraction. Any observer without inference could recognize record keeping, selling, customer servicing, agent training, and so forth in the context of a life insurance branch office. In this study, direct observation of first-line supervisors at work for long, continuous periods is supplemented by interviews of the first-line supervisors, their peers, superiors, and subordinates. This data-gathering approach helped the researcher minimize the bias introduced into the first-line supervisor's behavior by the researcher's presence because it permitted multiple opportunities for verification of observations. The incidence and time consumed in each activity are the important dimensions.

"Interaction" shall mean "an occurrence involving two or more people in which the actions of one person stimulate a reaction by another (or others)."[7] The stimulus may be a gesture, a word, or a note, but the contact must be direct—though not necessarily face to face. If the stimulus is transmitted from A to C through B, there is no interaction between A and C. The important dimensions here are the frequency of contact, the duration of contact, and the initiation pattern (who goes to whom). The researcher employed the same data-gathering methodology for interactions as he did for activities.

"Sentiments" shall represent feelings and attitudes as widely defined by Homans[8] and Guest.[9] Here, however, this researcher does not report what Guest calls "expressed feelings." More properly, this sentiment data is observed-expressed feelings. Basically, the researcher inferred sentiments from observed behavior. Sometimes the researcher probed for expressed feelings after observing behavior; other times, "expressed feelings" prompted observation. (An example of this latter-type sentiment would be the following: A first-line supervisor told the researcher he felt dominated by his superior.

---

[6]Homans, *op. cit.*, p. 34.
[7]Guest, *op. cit.*, p. 83.
[8]Homans, *op. cit.*, p. 38.
[9]Guest, *op. cit.*, p. 92.

The researcher later observed this man's superior many times by-pass the first-line supervisor to have direct supervisory contact with an agent. In almost all the first-line supervisor's many contacts with his superior the superior initiated the interaction.) In any case, sentiment data does not have the same character of directly observed evidence as do activities and interactions. However, the advantage to the observed-expressed sentiment data is that the reader can make his own judgment about validity and reliability of the inferences by checking the observed behavior reported in each case. Insistence on this type of data does reduce somewhat the richness of sentiment detail, but experience in a number of industrial attitude surveys has made the researcher skeptical of the scientific value of "expressed feeling" data, particularly when the number of respondents is small. Such data may still have some value in the policy system when used by the proper manager.

By so defining activities, interactions, and sentiments the researcher has descriptive categories to classify observed behavior. One "piece" of behavior could provide data for all three categories. The categories, as different modes of behavior, facilitate analytic description that can stand up to the tests of validity and reliability in clinical case studies. It is the judgment of the researcher that, given the nature of the behavior (actual and proposed) under study, stopwatch[10] or interaction-chronograph[11] precision would not have contributed to the scientific value of the data. Data in this form would have permitted statistical manipulation and statistical tests, but the gain in reliability would have been overbalanced by the loss in validity in these particular circumstances. "While *reliability* refers to the adequacy of operational techniques, *validity* refers to the extent to which the operation approximates the theoretical idea which the investigator is interested in studying; and these two tend to be inversely related."[12] The less formal observational technique used in this study minimized the "Hawthorne effect" and preserved the non-threatening atmosphere fostered by the researcher's independent role. The branch office personnel were especially wary of the more formal

[10] See especially the studies cited by Robert Dubin, "Business Behavior Behaviorally Viewed," in Argyris, *et al.*, *Social Science Approaches to Business Behavior*, ed. Strather, George B. (Homewood, Ill.: Richard D. Irwin, Inc., and the Dorsey Press, 1962) .

[11] See Eliot D. Chapple, "The Interaction Chronograph: Its Evolution and Present Applications," *Personnel*, XXV (1949) , 295–307.

[12] Mechanic, David, "Some Considerations in the Methodology of Organization Studies," in *The Social Science of Organizations*, ed. Leavitt, Harold J. (Englewood Cliffs, N.J.: Prentice-Hall, Inc., 1963) , 142.

procedures at the time of this research because this study coincided with a work measurement project for the clerical staff. The situation called for what may be referred to as a macroanalysis of behavior rather than a microanalysis.

The difference can be exemplified in the recording of the following event, first a macropresentation, than a micropresentation: (1) The first-line supervisor spent 5 percent of his workweek in office training a new agent, initiating the whole interaction. (2) The first-line supervisor speaks for 11.5 minutes; 0.5 minute pause; writes on board for 2.5 minutes; 0.5 minute pause; speaks for 1.0 minute; 0.75 minute pause; agent speaks 2.75 minutes; first-line supervisor interrupts and speaks for 4.5 minutes; and so forth.

The researcher is fortunate to have had a check on the correspondence of these data to the real world from the insurance company officers and the consultants involved. In addition to the submission of this written document to both parties, the researcher has spent almost 24 hours of oral feedback sessions with these informed critics.

SUMMARY

This clinical case study of a management consultant assisting an insurance company client through a major reorganization should begin to fill the gap in our understanding of the full range of change agent behaviors. By design the description of the change process is separated from the researcher's attempts to explain and evaluate what happened. For this reason, we can be bolder about the judgments we finally make about the planning and controlling of organizational change.

In the next chapter the "before" side of the before-and-after picture begins to take shape. We see the men in the positions crucial to the reorganization—the first line supervisors in the several hundred insurance company branch offices—behaving in their accustomed manner prior to the reorganization.

CHAPTER THREE

Assistant Manager Behavior before Conversion

WHAT THE CONSULTANTS SAW

IN THE COURSE of the diagnostic phase of the consulting engagement in mid-1961, a team of three consultants visited 22 branch offices (a representative sample, but less than 10 percent of the total number) in eight states across the country. They observed and interviewed 45 first-line supervisors[1] as well as other personnel in the branches. After reading the consultants' notes and reports and after extended discussion with them, the researcher expressed what the consultants saw of assistant manager behavior in terms of the categories described in the second chapter.

Assistant Managers' Activities

The assistant managers spent upward of 75 percent of their workweek in "demonstration selling." Though this activity tended to be outright selling in support of an agent, it was, more often than not, low-level training of the "watch-me-and-learn" variety. Typically, a perfunctory planning session on Friday afternoon set up the following week's work. Assistant manager and agent met in the agent's territory at around 9 AM on Monday to begin prospecting ("cold" canvassing or following up on direct mail and/or telephone solicitation). Such would be the agenda until mid- or late afternoon when the two would generally part for supper at home. Back together

---

[1]This number included men who would later become regular managers and those who were to become special managers, the former outnumbering the latter three to one. Under the old system, regular as well as special agents generally served together under an assistant manager (first-line supervisor) in undifferentiated work groups.

again at about 6:30 PM, they would follow up sales leads for as long as three hours.

Tuesday would follow the same pattern except that "demonstration selling" usually began two to three hours later. Wednesday matched the Monday pattern, as did Thursday, except for a shorter afternoon in the field for the assistant manager. Seldom was there "demonstration selling" activity on Friday, Saturday, or Sunday. In a "normal" week, then, the assistant manager would spend about 30 hours with one agent in the field doing "demonstration selling."

Diverse activities occupied the balance of the "normal" week. Conservation[2] activity—half the time with an agent and half the time alone—kept the assistant manager in the field for about two hours more at random times during the week. In-office activities consumed 20 percent of the assistant manager's time. On Tuesday and Friday mornings he spent about two hours processing the reports of his staff (averaging between seven and eight agents), each day requiring of each man a report of production and conservation. The assistant manager spent 7 to 8 percent of his normal week attending two meetings, for the most part as a listener. On Thursday afternoon, the first-line supervisors (averaging three per branch office) met as a group with the branch manager. It was at this time the assistant manager received his next week's assignment. On Friday morning the first-line supervisors assisted at the general branch office meeting conducted by the branch manager. While it was more common for the branch manager to "handle the whole show," in some cases the assistant manager was offered a "bit part," usually in the educational section of the meeting. Finally, 2 to 3 percent of his time was spent in office detail—processing mail, updating branch progress boards, preparing his report Form 09, and so forth.

The "normal" week's activity pattern predictably accommodated to peak loads monthly and annually. Each month, just before monthly lapses had to be reported, the time consumed in conservation doubled and even trebled at the expense of "demonstration selling" time. Toward the end of each year, the workweek many times was lengthened and selling activities intensified. The whole branch office strained to accumulate the credits that were totaled at year's end for recognition rewards.

Other periodic or nonprogrammed activities altered the "normal" week. Each assistant manager could almost plan on teaching the

---

[2]Preventing life-insurance policies from lapsing because of nonpayment of premiums.

"Career Extension Course" for the new agents once every two years (two hours a week each week for six months). He could also plan on replacing his usual "demonstration selling" time with auditing time for each of the agents on his staff at least every 18 months (two weeks per agent of verifying accounts by visiting policyholders and by auditing the agent's account book). Less predictable but more disruptive were the activities associated with agent terminations and appointments. Termination called for an audit of the agent's accounts. In the period from termination to new appointment, the assistant manager had to collect and service the accounts in the vacant territory. These activities would normally take up to 50 percent of the "demonstration selling" time. The termination-appointment cycle was complete only when the assistant manager spent three to four weeks introducing the new appointee—teaching bookkeeping procedures, showing him the territory and collection procedures, training him to prospect and sell by "demonstration selling." Given the turnover ratio of agents, each assistant manager could expect to go through at least one termination-introduction cycle each year.[3] The degree of interruption to the "normal" week activity pattern is determined by the length of time between termination and introduction. Assistant managers in each branch usually bear an equal burden of these periodic activities at the direction of the branch manager.

Assistant Managers' Interactions

In the "normal" week, the assistant manager spent 85 percent of his time with individual agents. About 60 percent of that time, assistant manager and agent were in the company of prospective customers. Of the remainder, about 15 percent was time spent together in the field, while 10 percent was spent at the assistant manager's desk in the branch office. Interaction in the field is normally with the same agent for two successive weeks. The periods together are long. The assistant manager initiates the field interaction as a whole.[4] The interaction with agents in the office consists of a 10- to 15-minute session with each member of the assistant manager's staff twice a week. Here, too, the assistant manager is the initiator.

---

[3] A territory temporarily vacant through agent disability also burdens the assistant manager with the collection and servicing responsibilities.

[4] A microanalysis of such extended interactions reveals the shifting initiation of normal conversation, but given the activity occasioning the interaction ("demonstration selling") the supervisor dominates the interaction. Only where a microanalysis of such extended interactions adds a significant insight will it be detailed here.

While the assistant managers assist at meetings together for 10 percent of their "normal" workweek, there is no programmed interaction between them.

The interaction during this 10 percent of the "normal" week is really between the branch manager and the assistant manager in a group context. These interactions are programmed for twice a week. The branch manager is initiator. Branch manager and assistant manager interact through a combined assignment-report form (Form 09) once a week, with the assistant manager initiating the report phase.

The assistant manager has only infrequent and random interactions with the clerical staff on business matters.

Assistant Managers' Sentiments

The two most important sentiments were the assistant manager's attitude toward his job and his attitude toward the agents on his staff. First, the assistant manager viewed his position not as a career but as a stepping stone. He knew his financial rewards were modest compared to the branch manager's. Generally he knew that his earnings amounted to less than half of what the branch manager earned and that he had little prospect of reaching income levels over $10,000 (only 13.4 percent were able to achieve that in 1960). He felt—and the record shows—that he was quite mobile. (Attrition was trending upward. More than one in ten left the job each year. Only 18 percent of the 1961 attrition was for promotion; 53 percent returned to the agent level; 29 percent was terminations.)

The assistant manager saw himself more as a supersalesman than a supervisor. He was more interested in showing a fine record of production from his "demonstration selling" on the Form 09 than he was in developing the seven or eight men assigned to his staff. Loyalty to company and branch office was strong, but staff allegiance was virtually nonexistent. The assistant manager felt a sense of responsibility in carrying out the specific assignments given him each week by the branch manager, but he felt little responsibility on a continuing basis for any agent or any group of agents on his staff.

PRECONVERSION ASSISTANT MANAGER BEHAVIOR IN BRANCHES 7 AND 8

The researcher made his own observations and interviews in branches 7 and 8 and found the consultants' generalized view of the assistant managers in the sample of 45 to be essentially accurate. The seven first-line supervisors in these two offices generally fitted the profile of the average first-line supervisor (age, length of service, earnings, etc.). The behavior patterns presented in detail here are those of Assistant Managers 7A, 7B, 8A, and 8B. (The researcher was able to spend the most time with these four.) In each case a workweek is described and comments are made to indicate how typical the observed behavior is in the eyes of the man himself, his superior, peers, and subordinates.

Activities of Individual Assistant Managers

Activities—7A. This supervisor's activity pattern differed from the "normal" week observed by the consultants chiefly because of the nonprogrammed activity of new agent introduction that took 40 percent of 7A's time. "Demonstration selling" by 7A, when he was with a relatively new agent, more resembled training than outright selling *for* the agent. "You watch me with this prospect, because the next one is yours." 7A consistently conducted a postmortem after each call with the newer agent. On three of the four evenings of "demonstration selling" 7A worked with a relatively new agent. Three times during the week, special agents on 7A's staff asked him to accompany them on appointments with special clients. He spent 7 percent of his time so occupied. 7A spent less time in formal meetings than the typical assistant manager profiled by the consultants. The branch manager held no formal meeting on Thursday with his first-line supervisors. During the Friday morning general meeting, 7A participated to the extent that he ran the projector for a filmstrip. Most of the in-office miscellaneous activity was information exchange with clerks, the branch manager, and the researcher. An hour was spent alone readying the filmstrip and materials for distribution at the general meeting. About 60 percent of 7A's time was consumed in in-office activities.

Had it not been for the in-office training time spent with the new agent, the observed behavior would have been typical of 7A's usual pattern. Normally that time would have been spent in "demonstration selling." It was more customary, too, for 7A to give a presentation at the general meeting—usually a 10-minute educational talk. The branch manager said, "I just couldn't find a spot for him in this week's program."

Activities—7B. This first-line supervisor conformed more closely to the "normal" week schedule of activities observed by the consultants. He spent 60 percent of his time in "demonstration selling" or conservation with one of his agents during five days and four nights. In-office programmed activities were the two-hour general meeting, during which he gave a 15-minute presentation on a new health plan, and the four hours spent in processing the agent's biweekly reports. In addition to these in-office activities, about an hour and a half a day were spent in "office detail"—a rubric covering a wide range of activities (opening mail, processing a death claim, tracking down an error on a home office report form, receiving instructions from the branch manager, helping an agent find an error in his bookkeeping, preparing his presentation for the general meeting, etc.)—intertwined with continuous, business-oriented small talk. A 20- to 30-minute trip to the coffee shop was ritualistic each morning and occurred on two afternoons also.

Interviews indicated this pattern was typical. Office detail was not so much associated with his position as with his obvious willingness to talk "the business" and lend a hand. Agents and branch manager alike took advantage of this trait.

Activities—8A. "Demonstration selling" accounted for 57 percent of 8A's workweek. Though no nonprogrammed activities interfered with the "normal" workweek, habit developed over 25 years in this position tied this man to the office and prevented virtually all (in this week, all) night work. Of the 43 percent of his time spent in the office, 12 percent was occupied by report processing, 10 percent by passive meeting attendance (8A spoke to the general group on Friday for just over 20 minutes about a sales incentive campaign), and 21 percent by "office detail." The activities in this final catchall category consumed about one and a quarter hours a day. Included were such tasks as processing his daily mail, reading home office circulars, collecting sealed bids from the agents for excess office furniture, moving boxes of supplies, and preparing his general meeting presentation.

Peers and subordinates insisted the above distribution of time was generally typical, if somewhat overstated in the proportion of field time. Supervisor 8B complained that 8A was "making only a 10 percent effort for his equal share of the branch incentive." Both sources said 8A's workweek was appreciably shortened by his avoidance of night work. Neither could account for the time spent on office detail except to blame it on "paper shuffling."

Activities—8B. Nonprogrammed tasks prevented this first-line supervisor from acting according to the pattern identified as the "normal" workweek by the consultants. One old-timer on his staff had been seriously ill for two months, and a second man had broken a leg three weeks earlier. Among the seven well men was an agent who had returned the week previous from new agents' school. It so happened in this week, also, that 8B was ill on one of the days for agent "check-off"—the day, too, when the management meeting was held. As a result his behavior pattern is quite different. (Unpredictable peak loads of unprogrammed activities often burdened the first-line supervisors in branch offices. The difference here is that the branch manager did not distribute the work load among 8A, 8B, 8C, and 8D, as was the general rule elsewhere.)

This supervisor's activity pattern comes very close to what would be standard for a regular agent. Virtually all the daylight hours of Monday, Wednesday, and Thursday were occupied riding and then walking from door to door, collecting weekly or monthly premiums due in the two disability agencies. Bookkeeping and processing of mail payments took slightly less than one hour for each four hours in the field. Field activities associated with the two disability agencies were rounded out with two hours of customer contact on Friday in an effort to conserve business. On Wednesday and Thursday evenings 8B spent a total of three hours with his new agent in "demonstration selling." Aside from the bookkeeping and mail processing, in-office activities took just 14 percent of his time. Most of Friday morning was spent in processing agent reports and in passively attending the general meeting. On Thursday morning 8B spent about an hour trying to prove the home office had erred in denying one agent on his staff a recognition award for 1963. This activity was a composite of record search, computation, discussion, and letter writing.

Except for the day's illness, this activity pattern was typical for 8B for the past three months. Open or disability agencies had eaten up the time usually spent in "demonstration selling." All interviewees agreed that 8B in normal times had spent at least three quarters of an unusually long workweek in the field with agents.

Interactions of Individual Assistant Managers

Interactions—7A. First-line supervisor 7A spent 84 percent of his time with individual agents: 40 percent with one new agent in extended periods of teacher-student type interactions where 7A was initiator, 19 percent with another agent in two and a half hour sessions on three different evenings—7A again the initiator—8 percent with still another agent in like circumstances, 7 percent with two different agents in interactions (averaging one and a half hours each) initiated by the agents, and 10 percent in 7A-initiated brief, deskside sessions with each of the eight men on the staff twice during the week. Interactions with the branch manager averaged five a day but consumed just a little more than an hour in total during the whole week. Most of the time 7A initiated the contact, but in virtually every case the exchange saw both parties as initiators. 7A was the responder in the general meeting interaction conducted by the branch manager. Interactions with the clerks were very similar to the contacts with the branch manager in duration and type. Daily social amenities alone dictated the interactions between 7A and his peers, the other two first-line supervisors.[5]

Interactions—7B. Contact with individual agents occupied 85 percent of 7B's time: 60 percent with one agent in long interactions over the five days and evenings, 10 percent with the eight members of his staff in the short, biweekly "check-off," 15 percent with agents at random (including all but six agents in the office). The initiation pattern on all but these random contacts was that of first-line supervisor to agent. In these last contacts, agents initiated almost half. Their duration varied from two or three minutes to a half hour, and often what started as a two-person interaction grew to a five- or six-person "bull session." All but one of the ten interactions with the branch manager were initiated by 7B, who consistently spent more time in each contact with his superior than did 7A. Three of the seven trips to the coffee shop involved prolonged interaction with the branch manager. In peer interaction, also, 7B differed from 7A. The former initiated two in-office discussions of a half hour each with 7C and joined 7C three times in the coffee shop. 7B had substantially the same interaction pattern with the clerical force that 7A did.

Interactions—8A. About 70 percent of 8A's time was spent with individual agents: 57 percent with one man in relatively long daylight interactions during four days, 12 percent in the biweekly check-off of each of his nine agents, the remainder when a dozen different agents came to him with sealed bids. This first-line supervisor initiated all but these last very brief, nonrecurring contacts. 8A in-

---

[5]These fleeting contacts will not be considered as interactions since no bona fide response was identifiable.

teracted with the branch manager twice during the week, in a group
with his three peers and in the relatively brief portion of the general
meeting conducted by the branch manager. The management meeting lasted an hour and a half; 8A was a responder the whole time.
He responded, too, when 8D assigned him his role in the general
meeting. Peer interactions were few (four with two of his three
peers), brief, except for the two coffee-shop sessions, and consistently
initiated by others. At the general meeting 8A did seize the initiative
for almost one fifth of the time. Three fifths of this general meeting
was conducted by 8C and 8D.

Interactions—8B. In sharp contrast to the other patterns identified here, 8B spent only 13 percent of his time with individual
agents: 5 percent in the brief check-off sessions with the seven men
on his staff and 8 percent in two extended interactions with one
agent—all initiated by 8B. He also initiated the only interaction he
had with the branch manager outside of the general meeting. In the
course of this 15-minute contact, the branch manager seized the
initiative, so that 8B ended up as responder. Peer interaction consisted in about a 30-minute discussion session with 8C and 8D,
initiated by 8B, and almost two hours of responder role at the general
meeting. The bookkeeping and mail-processing activities involved
8B in numerous but brief contacts with the clerical staff, almost all
initiated by 8B.

Sentiments of Individual Assistant Managers

Sentiments—7A. This man announced with vigor that his goal
was to be a branch manager—soon! The "hungry young Turk"
appellation was given him by superior, subordinates, and peers. His
eagerness to record volume on Form 09 brought him some strong
criticism for pirating prospects from others and for "paper-hanging."[6]
He had already completed one part of the five-part CLU course,
leading to the degree he perceived as a criterion for promotion. He
perceived also that association with special agents, instead of regular
agents, would give him more "visibility" (his word), and he continually pressed the researcher for confirmation on this point. In
this attitude, then, he fit the profile drawn by the consultants. However, 7A's supersalesman activities left room for a sense of responsi-

---

[6]Putting business on the books that could be preserved only with the utmost
difficulty by the collecting or servicing agent.

bility for the agents on his staff. He enjoyed a fine reputation as a trainer. His handling of the new agent during the week of observation was thorough to the point of being "nit-picking." He said, "Last year I forced a man out of the business just by riding herd on him." This could not be verified,·but the researcher was present when 7A told the branch manager that he wanted to get rid of special agent 7A7. He prided himself that the staff he had last year led the office and that this year—though he was assigned last year's "leper colony" —he was again leading the office. His agents reported that within the month he had treated them to a stag party at his home.

Sentiments—7B. It had been eight years since 7B was promoted to first-line supervisor. He had seen a man who started with him in the business 15 years ago progress rapidly to become the branch manager in branch 7. Superior, subordinates, peers, and 7B himself spoke as if promotion opportunities for 7B were past. He seemed resigned, if somewhat disappointed. He had done nothing about getting his CLU degree. In the researcher's presence he asked the assistant regional manager if there was any chance that one of the first-line supervisors could be officially appointed assistant branch manager (an office not in use anywhere in the company). For some time 7B had been unofficially carrying the ball during the periodic absences of the branch manager. With this modification, 7B seemed ready to accept his current position as a career position. Also in contrast to 7A, 7B identified more with the office as a whole instead of his own eight-man staff. At one time or other he had supervised virtually every man in the office. He interacted, both initiating and reacting, with almost every agent without discrimination. Agents, no matter what staff they were on, felt free to—and often did—seek his help as a specialist in the accounting end of the business.

Sentiments—8A. With a little more than five years to serve before retirement, 8A had no expectations for promotion. His family was raised and educated. During his 27-year tenure as first-line supervisor (not unprecedented but relatively rare in the company) he had seen more than a dozen peers come and go (most returned to the agent status, two of whom were on 8A's present staff). However, he fit the consultants' profile of the first-line supervisor in the other attitude. He felt little responsibility for the agents on his staff. He boasted to the researcher of treating his men tough. At no time was this more evident than during the biweekly check-off sessions. His manner was brusk, and his voice was often raised in criticism or blame. The agents on his staff generally resented his "agent-be-damned" attitude and often expressed their feelings. The researcher witnessed a high-decibel verbal exchange between 8A and one of his older agents in full view of the entire agent force. Some agents did attest to 8A's unmatched ability to train agents in the accounting side of the business, but five agents had informed the branch manager of their unwillingness to serve on 8A's staff.

Sentiments—8B. This man, while scarcely 35 years old and less than four years in the position, expressed no interest in promotion. More accurately, he felt there was no chance of promotion—largely because no one had been promoted from branch 8 in the last 20 years. Rather than study for the CLU degree, he went one night a week to a local college for a course in the psychology of human relations to learn more "about motivating the agents." Given the practice of the branch manager of assuming each first-line supervisor took care of his own staff, 8B had developed a strong sense of responsibility for his nine agents. In the week before the researcher's visit 8B had asked 8C to service the two disability agents for two days so that he could give his new agent a solid two days of introduction. During the week of observation, 8B went out two nights with his new agent after the exhausting effort of collecting all day. In addition, 8B was building a playroom in his cellar so he could have staff parties—reported by both 8B and agents on his staff. Other agents in the office asked specifically to get on 8B's staff, and he generally had the reputation of being willing to do even the unreasonable to help his men.

SUMMARY

The consultant's generalized picture of the first-line supervisor's normal workweek behavior, based on a sample of forty-five men in twenty-two branch offices, does not resemble what is normally thought of as a supervisory pattern. Under normal conditions, he is more supersalesman than supervisor. This general conclusion is supported by the observations made of the four first-line supervisors in branches 7 and 8. What these latter observations dramatically point up, in comparison to the consultant's composite picture, is that non-programmed activities substantially modified this normal workweek pattern. Unpredictable terminations or disabilities drastically alter the normal workweek.

The activity time of the first-line supervisor is, under normal conditions, usually taken up largely by "demonstration selling"—actually soliciting business for agents. Such activity takes place in large, uninterrupted, blocks of time. But for the reporting and meeting schedule, his week is unstructured by work flow or schedule. In the summary table of first-line supervisor activity in Exhibit 3–1, the differences observed by consultant and researcher are largely explained by the nonprogrammed events mentioned above. Were it not for these events, the patterns would be very similar except for the disproportionate amount of time spent on office detail by 7B and 8A. These latter differences may be best explained by the relative age and tenure of these two men. Both men were older and had spent longer time in the position than the company average.

EXHIBIT 3–1
Summary of Observed Assistant Manager Activities
Percent of Workweek Spent in Various Activities

Activities	Consultant's Observations of 45 Assistant Managers	7A	Researcher's Observation of Assistant Managers 7B	8A	8B
Demonstration selling	75%	34%	60%	57%	8%
Conservation	5				5
Processing agent reports	10	10	10	12	5
Group meetings	7–8	5	5	10	5
Office detail	2–3	7	19	21	4
Socializing		4*	6		
Collecting agency					57
Bookkeeping					16
In-office training		40			

*Professional meeting.

The interaction patterns observed by the consultant and the researcher are very similar—see Exhibit 3–2. Most of the first-line supervisor's time is spent in individual contact with agents, virtually always initiated by the first-line supervisor. 8B's departure from the normal pattern is caused by the necessity to perform almost as an agent in filling in for disabled agents on his staff. 8A's relatively advanced age probably explains his departure from the norm. Note that normally the first-line supervisor is almost never alone. Virtually all his interactions are verbal, extended contacts, initiated by him.

EXHIBIT 3–2

Summary of Observed Assistant Manager Interactions

Percent of Workweek Interacting with Various People

Interacting with	Consultant's Observations of 45 Assistant Managers	Researcher's Observations of Assistant Managers			
		7A	7B	8A	8B
Individual agents	85%	84%	85%	70%	13%
Group of agents			< 1	< 1	
Branch manager alone	< 1	3	5		< 1
Branch manager in group	7–8	5	4	6	< 1
Peer alone			5	< 1	
Peer in group				7	5
Clerks	1	< 1	< 1	< 1	2
Home office					< 1

Significantly, though, he is the responder in almost all of his interactions with his immediate superior. Such interactions are brief and limited (in total time). Peer contact is even more limited and casual than contact with his superior.

First-line supervisor sentiments match in both the consultant's and researcher's samples. He sees himself not as a supervisor so much as a supersalesman whose task it is to further demonstrate selling ability to be promoted. The assistant manager position, then, is a half-way house on the road from agent status to branch manager status. He feels little responsibility for the half dozen or more agents on his staff. Instead, he identifies more with the branch office as a whole.

Such is the typical behavior pattern of the first-line supervisor before the recommendations made by the consultant. Before going on with the description of the consulting process, it is important to inquire what accounted for this particular type of behavior pattern of the assistant manager. An understanding of the forces molding his behavior will permit a more in-depth appreciation of the changes to come. The next chapter details the basic influences on assistant manager behavior as of the first quarter of 1961.

CHAPTER FOUR

Basic Influences on Assistant Manager Behavior as of the First Quarter of 1961

INTRODUCTION

THE INSURANCE COMPANY that provided the setting for this research could be profiled as follows: an almost 100-year-old mutual life-insurance company with assets in excess of $10 billion, serving over 20 million policyholders with over 30,000 employees in a central home office and several hundred branch offices. In and around the company at the beginning of 1961 were numerous variables affecting the behavior of the first-line supervisor. It will be helpful to group these variables under three headings: environmental, structural, and behavioral. The treatment of the variables under each heading will include a description of the character of the variables and an indication of how the variables affected the behavior of the first-line supervisor. The treatment has been particularized for branches 7 and 8 where there were significant differences in the influences shaping assistant manager behavior. It was from the researcher's observations in branches 7 and 8 and from the consultant's observations in 22 branches that this material was developed.

ENVIRONMENTAL CONTEXT

External Economics

A look at the buyer's side of the market reveals a demand increase that has outstripped the rate of population growth since World War

II. Insurance in force has grown fivefold in that time, with life-insurance agents adding almost $50 billion net a year in new business.[1] The character of postwar demand showed signs of shifting. Income distribution had changed so that the fastest-growing segment of the population was the group earning more than $7,000. White-collar occupations had grown faster than blue-collar occupations. Population growth had been spread unevenly nationally and in different patterns than in prewar times. Within metropolitan areas, decay had hit city centers while the suburbs boomed. The more dynamic market was made up of people who tended to pay their premiums by mail on receipt of a notice rather than give the cash weekly or monthly to a collecting agent. Even the rate of change in these market characteristics had increased.[2] The response of the company under study had not been complete enough to keep it in phase with the market trends. Its traditional market niche was erod-ing.

On the seller's side of the market, competition had been stiffening all through the 1950's. The number of companies competing almost trebled in the decade, most of the increase coming among stock com-panies.[3] The latter increased their market share about 10 percent in the decade at the expense of the mutual companies. Other institu-tions competed for the "savings" dollar and did appreciably better in the decade 1950–60 than did life-insurance company reserves and time deposits in mutual savings banks, which both increased by about 80 percent. Total assets of open-end mutual funds grew almost sevenfold, and accounts of individuals in savings and loan associa-tions increased almost four and a half times.

Finally, in the human resources aspect of the market, the demand for good agents exceeded the supply. Entry was easy and mobility was very good.

External Economics of Branches 7 and 8 in Particular. Both branches were in the same high income and growing market area, the first serving a suburban-rural territory, the second a suburban-urban territory. All the trends in the buyer's side of the market identified above fit these branches. On the seller's side, the company

────────

[1]"The Great Boom in Life Insurance Stocks," *Forbes* (April 15, 1964), 21.

[2]From the consultant's report.

[3]Whereas mutual companies can write only participating policies—obligating them to share through dividends at least some of the operating gains with the policyholders—the stock companies almost always issue nonparticipating policies, allowing the stock-holders to be the sole beneficiaries of operating gains.

under study held a shrinking lead in market share of new business and insurance in force. The stiff competition was probably most evident in the manpower aspect of the market. The men who were best fitted to sell in the expanding part of the market could choose from any one of a dozen giant firms or innumerable smaller firms or they could go into the independent general agency section of the market.

Institutional Setting

One feature of the life-insurance industry affects all companies alike. The industry is highly regulated by individual state, not federal, bodies. The range of regulation rigor is very broad and, hence, proliferation of companies in the past decade was centered in two or three states. Since these state bodies regulate differently the amount of allowable expenses per $1,000 of premium income and legislate differently a maximum of first-year and total commissions, a company domestic to a "strict" state can be disadvantaged when competing as a foreign company in other states with companies domestic to more "lenient" states. This situation affects the competition for good agents with the lure of higher first-year and/or total commissions.

The industry is so structured that the agent has opportunity for extracompany professional and educational exposure. In most states the agents have a quasi-professional trade association, one of whose important functions is to voice agent sentiment to the state regulation body. In the educational sphere certain courses of study and degrees (CLU and LUTC,[4] for instance) are nationally recognized and have significant status.

A final institutional factor is the agents' union, which holds a minority position nationally and in the company under study (in this company, one third of the agents work under a union contract while only 10 percent pay dues). In 1961 this company lived under an arrangement wherein the union had to win certification state by state, not branch by branch.

Institutional Setting and Branches 7 and 8 in Particular. The only comment needed here refers to the unionization of agents. Agents were nonunion in both branches and there was no active

---

[4]Chartered Life Underwriters and Life Underwriter Training Council.

organizing. (None of the data used in this study were drawn from a unionized setting.)

Internal Economics

The availability and utilization of financial, technological, and human resources were determinants of assistant manager behavior in the sense of being constraints. First, competitors argued, the net cost[5] position of this insurance company was worsening. More meaningfully, the margin above statutory expense allowances shrunk more than 8 percent in the years 1954–61. In this sense, efficiency in utilizing financial resources was trending down. At the same time, productivity per agent had remained constant. Among the top home office people the cost squeeze was causing concern. Cost was not a major concern, however, among the local branch managers or their subordinates.

The sales section of this company operated with essentially the same technology as its turn-of-the-century predecessors. The selling process still revolved about face-to-face customer contact—now a somewhat easier task with the proliferation of telephones and cars. Technological change had done nothing to facilitate the clerical burdens on the agent of recording, storing, transmitting, or retrieving data. In the branch offices the information system was a manual system. No other channel had replaced postal service as data transmission channel between branch and home office. In the home office departments servicing field sales, mechanization and automation were beginning to have an impact on data processing. As seen by the branch people, the new technology had not produced—and did not promise—any substantial changes in the sales function.

A final economic factor that is an uncontrollable (in the short run) constraint on the company as a whole is the profile of the human resources at each level. The profiles in Exhibit 4–1 are a composite of information on those newly appointed to each position in 1960. The total population in each position at the beginning of 1961 differs from the preceding most significantly among the regular agents and the assistant managers. The age distribution of all regular agents tended to be more normal, with the "over 50" group slightly

---

[5]Net cost is an often used—though questionable—relative measure of the cost of an insurance policy to the policyholder, considering premiums and dividends. It is based on uncertain future earnings and takes no account of the time value of money.

EXHIBIT 4–1

Composite Profile of 1960 Appointees
to Positions of Regular Agent, Special Agent,
Assistant Manager, and Branch Manager, in Percent

	Regular Agent	*Special Agent*	*Assistant Manager*	*Branch Manager*
Age				
24 and under	33	13	6	
25–29	29	30	33	26
30–34	18	25	30	
35–39	13	17	25	32
40 and over	7	15	6	42
Education				
College graduate	12	15	16	40
Attended college	34	32	33	23
High school graduate	41	38	41	37
Attended high school	13	15	10	0
Years with the company*				
Less than 1	40	7	0	0
1	17	40	9	0
2	11	29	34	0
3–4	14	11	33	0
5–10	13	7	23	39
11 and over	5	6	1	61

*In the case of regular agents, refers to years in last job.

outnumbering the "20–30" group. The average length of service among regular agents was about seven years, but the median was somewhat lower. The average pay for these men was slightly over $132 weekly. Pay in the larger urban areas was appreciably better than elsewhere—true for every position. The total population of assistant managers was significantly older than the new appointees. The average length of service, too, was higher in the total population. The assistant managers earned an average of $180 a week. The branch managers earned over $430 per week on the average. Turnover at the key assistant manager position was slightly over 10 percent (a third terminated, a little more than half returned to regular agent status, the balance were promoted).

The Internal Economics of Branches 7 and 8 in Particular. These branches varied from the general company picture in the following respects. Cost control in branch 8 was much worse than the company average, as was agent productivity. Branch 7 was slightly better than average in these respects. In terms of manpower, branch 7 was younger and newer to the business at all levels.

STRUCTURAL CONTEXT

For ease later on, these very important determinants of assistant manager behavior will be referred to as "systemic" variables.

Authority Structure

The personal life field sales division of the insurance company was formally structured as shown in Exhibit 4–2.

EXHIBIT 4–2
Preconversion Personal Life Sales Division

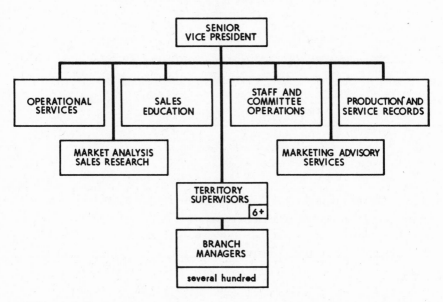

The company had a history of centralized policy formulation and administration. Also traditional was the exercise of functional authority by the home office staff groups—more highly specific procedural control than control by objectives or end results. The territory supervisors and their staffs operated from the home office, administering *à long* except for a visit to each branch about every year or 18 months.

The company had standardized the formal structure of each branch office without substantive change for three decades.

The branch manager shouldered full central line authority and was responsible for the following:

1. *Develop and Maintain a Sales Program*—Develop sales objectives based on capabilities of branch personnel and market potential; follow up individual performance and modify programs to meet changing conditions and to develop new markets.
2. *Recruit and Select Branch Personnel*—Employ people with the greatest potential for success.
3. *Train and Develop Branch Personnel*—Provide branch personnel with the knowledge and skills they require to perform their jobs well and to realize their own potential capabilities.
4. *Motivate Branch Personnel*—Build and maintain good human relations—to create in each of his people the will for personal success and the desire to contribute to the branch's success.
5. *Administer Office Detail*—Handle the administrative work that is required by the company.
6. *Develop and Maintain Good Public Relations*—Develop recognition of the company, its services and people, and build up his stature and that of his staff in the Life and Accident and Sickness insurance field.[6]

EXHIBIT 4–3
Preconversion Branch Office Organization

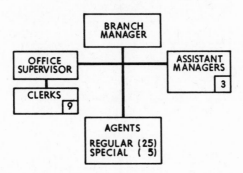

Except in the relatively rare case where an assistant manager headed a "detached office" (a satellite office serving a small market geographically distant from the branch), the company formally assigned the whole "ball of wax" to the branch manager. It would be true to say that his span of control embraced 35 men in the typical office described here.

The assistant manager position almost defies typing with classical management terms. In a qualified sense, the assistant manager position was a staff position. He did not have fixed and continuing super-

---

[6]From the branch manager's formal job description.

visory relationships with a group of subordinates. While the assistant manager was assigned a staff of seven to ten agents, this supervisory responsibility was limited to report checking twice a week. He had *ad hoc* delegations of functional authority over any one of the agents specified weekly or biweekly by the branch manager. Formally, all the assistant managers in a branch were peers. No official written job description existed for the assistant manager position.

The Authority Structure of Branches 7 and 8 in Particular

EXHIBIT 4–4
Branch 7 Organization

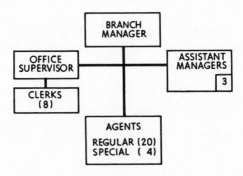

EXHIBIT 4–5
Branch 8 Organization

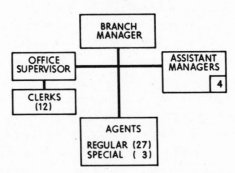

Reward Structure

The reward structure contained three elements: compensation, recognition, and promotion. The assistant manager received about 60 percent of his total income in fixed salary and 40 percent from "commission." Except for a small length-of-service increment, all assistant managers were assured the same minimum base. The fixed portion of the salary did depend on the volume of business in force in a particular branch, so in a high in-force branch the assistant managers could earn a higher base pay. In any one office each assistant manager received the same commission amount—a branch pool divided equally. The net volume of first-year commissions earned, the mix of policy types sold, and the record of conservation relative to average company performance determined the size of the branch pool (a system viewed as "too complex to figure out" by many of the management team). The assistant manager could and often did supplement his income by writing personal business and earning commissions directly. While some branch managers insisted that such business be given to agents, others allowed assistant manager to earn commissions of $1,000 or more a year. The branch manager, too, received about 60 percent of his income in a fixed salary. The size of this fixed base depended on the volume of insurance on the branch books. The variable portion of his income depended, as did the assistant manager's, on the volume of first-year commissions earned by the entire branch, the mix of policies sold, and the record of conservation. The consultant thought that this compensation formula, aside from its complexity, did not adequately reflect current results. The regular agent earned about 30 percent of his weekly income by collecting weekly and monthly premiums from shareholders. The balance of his income came from renewal and first-year commissions earned. The special agent depended entirely on renewal and first-year commissions.

A complex recognition system also affected the assistant manager's behavior. On a territorial basis, branch offices were ranked for their standing in sales trophy competition. So that all offices could compete regardless of size, standing was measured by a weighted composite index. The index included factors such as production per man per month, lapse rates, number of agents who have qualified for the Distinction Club or higher recognition awards, and controllable terminations. Performance on each was measured against average company performance on that factor. The home office monthly distributed the standings to each branch. In addition to the recognition achieved in sales trophy standing, branch management, including the assistant managers, annually strove to qualify the branch for the Distinction Club. Individual agents became eligible for the Distinction Club (two or three days at an extraoffice sales meeting) by earning at least a specified minimum of first-year commissions. A branch became eligible for the Distinction Club (thereby earning invitations for the assistant managers) when a specified proportion of the agents from the branch qualified as individuals or when the branch held a national standing in sales trophy competition among the top 25 percent or a territorial standing among the top 33 percent.

Though policy did not dictate promotion patterns, the route "up the ladder" varied little. Assistant managers moved up from the agent ranks after an average of three years. The next step, to sales education instructor, came usually after about four years as assistant manager. Working from the home office as sales education instructor or as part of the staff of the territorial supervisor occupied an average of five years more. The climb to the branch manager level took about 12 years in all. In the years 1958, 1959, and 1960, 60 percent of the new branch managers came from the sales education instructor ranks, 30 percent from the territorial supervisor's staff, and only 10 percent directly from the assistant manager position. Promote-from-within was the rule in this process. Almost without exception, too, was the practice of promoting within territories only. Since the pyramid narrowed so drastically above the branch manager position, these men generally bettered their positions by lateral moves to ever larger (measured by volume of insurance in force) branches.

In the selection for promotion at each level the company utilized a mix of criteria. Very high among the objective considerations was the individual's production record. The agent could offer the clearest evidence in terms of first-year commissions earned or volume of business placed.[7] The assistant manager could only show his weekly Form 09, which contained a record of new business written[7] with the agent on assignment. The sales education instructor used a form very much like the assistant manager's to record his production with various branch personnel as he traveled throughout the territory.

Reward Structure in Branches 7 and 8 in Particular.   There were two significant variations in branches 7 and 8 in the area of compensation. In branch 7 the assistant managers retained virtually no direct commissions for themselves, whereas in branch 8 the assistant managers derived about 10 percent of their income from this source. Branch 8 had a significantly higher volume of insurance in force.

---

[7]Insurance "placed" is a policy underwritten by the company and accepted by the customer. Insurance "written" is a policy in application form before underwriting.

Hence, the branch manager had a higher fixed base. In terms of sales trophy recognition, however, branch 7 stood close to the top in the territory while branch 8 fell toward the middle. Also, branch 7 rather consistently qualified enough agents so that the branch management could attend the Distinction Club. Branch 8 was much less consistent. The branches differed in promotion patterns, too. In over 20 years of branch 8's manager's tenure, no assistant manager had been promoted to sales education instructor. Three former assistant managers worked as agents in branch 8. One of the assistant managers was more than 20 years in the position; the three others averaged 4 years in the position. Three of the four were former agents in branch 8. Branch 7, on the other hand, had had three branch managers in the past nine years and as many assistant managers promoted in that time. No former assistant managers worked as agents. One assistant manager had spent 4 of his 12 years in this position; the other two each had been promoted a year and a half ago after serving as agents in other branches.

Work-Flow System and Schedule

The in-office work flow of the branch was tied directly to the field activity of the agents. The agent was engaged in prospecting, selling, collecting, and servicing. The selling activity generated a work flow involving only the branch office clerical staff and the underwriting and records sections of the home office. The collection activity also produced only a branch office clerical work flow in the normal course of events. Only when collections were in arrears did the assistant manager get involved in the work flow through his conservation efforts. Periodically the bookkeeping incident to the collection activity led to auditing tasks for the assistant manager. The agent's service activity only involved branch office clerical and home office work flow. The standard week's schedule was as follows: Tuesday morning, check-off and deposit; Friday morning, check-off, deposit, then branch office general meeting. During the check-off each agent in turn sat down next to the desk of the assistant manager on whose staff he served and reported on his selling and collecting activity. It was at this time that the assistant manager inquired about the conservation of policies in danger of lapsing. After the check-off, each agent waited in turn to deposit the money he had collected. The general meeting on Friday was intended for education, motivation, and recognition purposes. Time other than that indicated in the above schedule was unstructured (except for the meeting of branch and assistant managers usually held on Thursday afternoon).

The assistant manager's participation was critical to the work flow only in the juncture between selling-collecting and depositing because the company inserted the supervisory process of check-off. At the branch manager's direction, the assistant manager intervened at any and every stage of the agent work-flow activity to assist an established agent, to train a new agent, or to take a terminated or disabled agent's place.

Work-Flow System and Schedule in Branches 7 and 8 in Particular. Branches 7 and 8 did not deviate from the work flow or schedule as established by the company.

Information-Flow System

The assistant manager was not a key man in the structured flow of information. With only three exceptions the assistant manager did not send, receive, process, or store operational information. Most important for the assistant manager was Form 09, half of which he initiated in response to the branch manager's initiation of the other half. Weekly, the branch manager assigned the assistant manager his duties (time to be spent on what and with which agent). At the end of the week the assistant manager submitted—on the reverse side of the same form—his report of accomplishment on the assignment, usually measured in business "written" with the agent. This completed form, after review by the branch manager, was routed to the territory supervisor. In two other cases the assistant manager served as a clearing station for the agents on his staff for formal communications. Form 151, routed from the branch office clerks to the assistant manager, reported policyholders in arrears. The assistant manager used this in his supervision of conservation at check-off time. Form 174 was a request for an exemption—an agent asking to be relieved of responsibility for a particular policyholder's insurance because the policyholder had moved. The assistant manager processed these requests coming to and going from the agents on his staff.

All records of individual agent performance and pay were compiled by the branch office clerks under the direction of the branch manager, processed by the home office, and routed to the branch manager for storing. All business communications from the home office or from the territory supervisor were addressed to the branch manager. Annually, the branch manager submitted to the territory supervisor a set of branch objectives—usually stated as a projected absolute or percent increase in first-year commissions to be earned compared to the previous year—and, only rarely, an action plan to accomplish these objectives.

Physical Structure

Throughout the country, branch offices were very nearly standardized in layout and even in furnishings. The floor plan in Exhibit 4–6 depicts a small but growing branch office in which there were 17 regular agents, 4 special agents (room for 4 more), and 4 assistant managers. The following features of the office layout are worth noting. Special agents (a new position begun in the late 1950's) have their own offices, whereas regular agents work at their desks in an open room. Assistant managers work at desks in the regular agents' room too. In the wall separating the clerks' room from the regular agents' room there are mailboxes and service windows. It is at one of these that the agents made their biweekly deposits. The branch manager held the Friday morning general meetings in the regular agents' room.

Physical Structure in Branches 7 and 8 in Particular. Branches 7 and 8 were essentially no different from the physical structure pictured here. The diagrams in Exhibits 4–7 and 4–8 show the physical relationship among people in the two branches.

BEHAVIORAL CONTEXT

The behavior of those around the assistant manager significantly and relatively directly shaped the behavior pattern of the assistant manager.[8] Relying again on insights gained from the consultants and on the researcher's own observation in branches 7 and 8 prior to conversion, the following are the most significant elements of the branch manager's and agent's behavior patterns.

---

[8]The impression should not be given here that the assistant manager was only an adapter to forces, a passive element in the system. This study's focus on the assistant manager's behavior pattern as dependent variable should not and does not deny that the assistant manager himself could be and often was an active shaper of the system.

EXHIBIT 4-6
Typical Branch Office Floor Plan

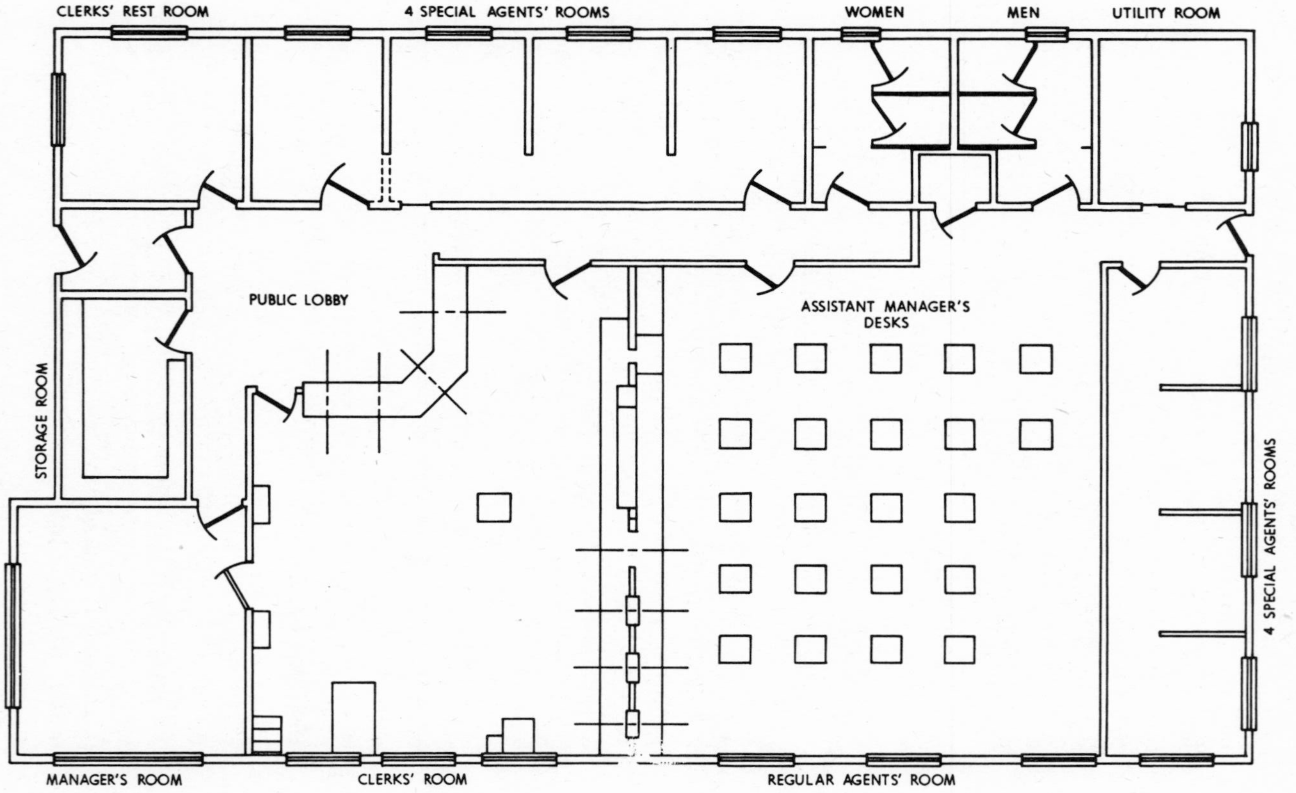

EXHIBIT 4-7
Branch 7—Regular Agents' Room

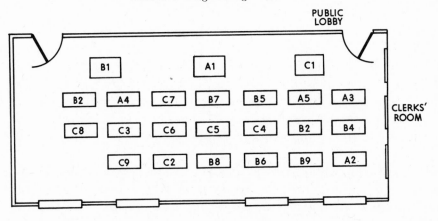

Note: Special agents A6, A7, A8, and A9 had semiprivate offices some 15 feet across the public lobby.

EXHIBIT 4-8
Branch 8—Regular Agents' Room

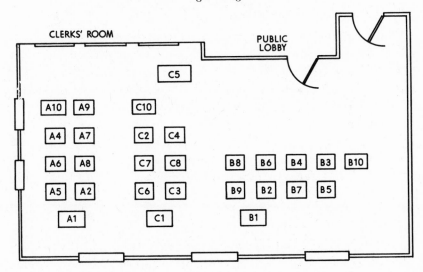

Note: Assistant Manager D1 and Special Agents D2, D3, and D4 had offices in another room some 50 feet across the public lobby.

The Branch Manager

The branch manager spent virtually all of his time in in-office *activities.* Record keeping and analysis of information consumed almost a quarter of his time. Responding to inquiries from office personnel, policyholders, and home office personnel occupied another quarter to a third of his time. Office work flow and schedule dictated a rather programmed set of activities that almost filled out the week. On Tuesday and Friday mornings during deposit and check-off time the branch manager often circulated in the agents' room, observing, making suggestions, congratulating, correcting, encouraging, and so forth. Thursday afternoon and Friday morning were taken up with the management meeting and the general meeting, respectively.

Almost half the branch manager's *interaction time* was spent with individual agents, the manager initiating about half the time. He spent about 5 percent more of his time interacting (initiating the greater share) with the agents and assistant managers as a group. An equal amount of time was similarly consumed with the assistant managers as a group. He initiated the majority of the oral contacts with home office personnel and the minority of written contacts. About half the latter was programmed information flow. Such extra-office interaction consumed 5 to 10 percent of his time. Leaving a quarter of his time for solitary activity, the branch manager divided the balance about equally among the clerks and policyholders, initiating about half the former and almost none of the latter.

The overriding *sentiment,* verbalized and acted out, was a sense of responsibility "for the whole show." The branch manager involved himself in every phase of the branch's affairs and wanted to be informed about the slightest detail. He felt important—peerless in an authority and social status sense. He was addressed as "Mister" by clerk and assistant manager alike, and he encouraged no broaching of like signs of deference. He was surrounded by unshared, differentiating appointments: wood-paneled and carpeted private office, personal stenographer, private phone, and so forth (the phones, the access to clerical aides, and the offices for special agents were recent innovations that still did not compare with the manager's facilities) .

In this area of sentiments, the consultants (who had the perspective and experience in the industry to make such a judgment) identified a value that was just about institutionalized in all levels of the company. There was a strong sense of stewardship responsibility based on the value position that forced savings is a social good. Emphasis on policyholder service and conservation of business was founded in this deep-seated conviction.

Branch Manager Behavior in Branches 7 and 8 in Particular.

Since the branch managers of branches 7 and 8 had heard—scarcely any official detail—of the impending changes recommended by the consultants, their behavior patterns were shifting somewhat prior to conversion. This appeared chiefly as a changing attitude toward the role of the assistant manager. Both branch managers felt inclined to let their assistants "carry the ball" a bit more, especially in general meetings. In both cases, too, the branch managers tended to give assignments to the assistants only with agents on their own staffs. However, for years it had been Branch Manager 8's practice to limit his agent contact to less than a quarter of the normal.

The Agents

Agent *activity* and its relationship to assistant manager behavior can be readily inferred from the work flow and schedule outlined above under "Work-Flow System and Schedule." One point that has not been specifically mentioned was the amount of office time, aside from the scheduled occasions on Tuesdays and Fridays, the agents spent in the office. Some geographically distant from the office came in only on those days. More generally, however, the agents came in to check the mail, pick up forms, do their daily bookkeeping after collecting, or just to socialize, sometimes with assistant managers. An hour spent in these activities on Monday, Wednesday, and Thursday would not be uncommon. Most often there would be a half dozen or more agents in the office in the early morning and the late afternoon.

One interesting fact about agent *interaction* should be noted here. Informal agent groups tended to exclude assistant managers. What might be peer groups were drawn from the whole agent population and were not limited by the staff boundaries. By observation and interview in branches 7 and 8, a number of such peer groups were identified (frequency of interaction, persistency of group composition at the coffee shop, references to card game cronies, social mixers, and cliques). Exhibits 4–9 and 4–10 are examples of such peer groups in branches 7 and 8.

One other point should be reinforced concerning the agents' interaction pattern. The agent brought his questions and problems to the branch manager first, and only after finding him unavailable sought out an assistant manager—not necessarily the one to whose staff he was assigned.

EXHIBIT 4–9
Peer Groups in Branch 7

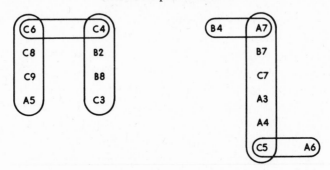

Note: By reference to Exhibit 4–7, see how the geographic proximity relates to peer groups when desk location is not made to conform to staff affiliation. Compare with the situation in branch 8 below and in Exhibit 4–8.

EXHIBIT 4–10
Peer Groups in Branch 8

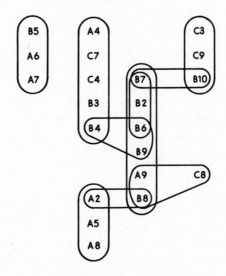

The assistant manager faced a range of important agent *sentiments.* The agent definitely held office allegiance over staff allegiance. He seldom thought of staff allegiance. Competition existed man to man, not staff to staff. The office tote board and the office bulletin reflected this fact. A second important sentiment concerned agent expectation of the assistant manager. The agent looked forward to the two-week assignment with the assistant manager as a boost to his sales total. Those having a poor quarter[9] or needing some business to qualify for the Distinction Club expected, and even requested the branch manager for, help (in putting business on the books) from the assistant manager. Agents could tell you who had not had an "assignment" in the last six months. Agents more often than not shared an attitude toward the assistant manager position itself. Many viewed promotion to this rank somewhat cynically. Many agents earned more as agents than as assistant managers. Also, some sensed that the assistant manager title did not ring true since the position was more supersalesman than supervisor. It was not unheard of for good (measured in terms of production) agents to turn down the promotion. It has been pointed out already that a large number of assistant managers returned to agent status each year (about half of the 10 percent turnover). The promotion-minded viewed the drawbacks of the position as sacrifices to be made on the road to the branch manager's chair. Finally, the agent who had some tenure with the company had a sense of loyalty and dedication and identified with the company to an extent unmatched in the researcher's business and consulting experience. A familial term of endearment was used with the company's name. Frankly, it took months of exposure to the culture to move the researcher from skeptic to agnostic to believer. Agents accepted the researcher's unfamiliar role almost without question when they heard he was cleared by the senior vice president and president. Often, in expressing a grievance, an agent would ask that the researcher convey the message "upstairs" because "they will remedy things if they know about them. They always have!" A surprising number wore company emblems of distinction or length of service pins at work each day. It may also be significant in this context that the agents had been slower to unionize in this company than in some others. What brought this sentiment into sharpest focus was the recurring theme: "Things are beginning to change." Very often, the agent—here specifically the regular agent—would disappointedly cite two recent examples where the company seemed to be acting out of character. One was the recent change in contract that affected the manner in which the agent's weekly pay was figured (pay changes every quarter on the basis of performance in the previous quarter). The agents perceived that the company had done this to even out the peaks and troughs in income, but the new system

---

[9]Pay varied only every quarter. The commissions earned in a 13-week period determined the pay for the next 13 weeks.

—it seemed to the agents—worsened the income swings. "I always thought the company would do nothing to hurt the agent, but . . . ." The second incident that seemed to have shaken the regular agent's confidence somewhat was the institution of the special agent status a few years ago. The latter were seen as getting preferential treatment and were feared as rivals—"They sell business right in my homes!" As was the case generally in the industry, status within the sales ranks was almost solely a function of production—volume of commissions earned. Membership in the Distinction Club, Special Distinction, or Millionaire Circle just about determined the pecking order. Special agent rank, with its distinguishing symbols, broke with this tradition. These examples were cited always with the prologue or epilogue: "I hope this doesn't mean the company is forgetting its agents!" Most agents sincerely did not want to believe the "evidence" but reflected a little hurt at the changes in a familial relationship. In fact, before these incidents, no significant change of any kind had been imposed on the agent for decades.

SUMMARY

This chapter has indicated the forces at work at the beginning of 1961 on the behavior of the assistant manager—the independent variables affecting the dependent variable. These forces in outline are as follows.

Environmental Context

External Economics—Shifts in the buyers' side of the market and proliferation of new competitors on the sellers' side made maintenance of market share difficult.

Institutional Setting—This is a highly regulated industry and one in which quasi-professional organizations are more important than unions.

Internal Economics—The firm under study was experiencing a worsening cost squeeze. Home office technological change had not spread to the branch offices. The existing manpower pool at the first-line supervisor level was relatively young, modestly paid, and subject to slightly more than a 10 percent annual turnover.

Structural Context

Authority Structure—The division under study had only three scalar levels but was operated with centralized procedural control.

Within each branch, the branch manager was responsible for "the whole ball of wax."

Reward Structure—The 40 percent of the first-line supervisor's pay that was "commission" came from a complex group incentive. Recognition, too, was a group-based reward. Promotion, based largely on sales ability, from agent to branch manager status took about 12 years.

Work-Flow System and Schedule—The branch work flow was designed to operate without first-line supervisor intervention except for two, relatively short, weekly supervisory activities. The balance of his involvement was on *ad hoc* assignment.

Information Flow System—The first-line supervisor had only an incidental role in the sending, receiving, processing, and storing of information.

Physical Structure—The branch office layout gave the first-line supervisor virtually no differentiating symbol. His desk, with those of the agent force, stood without partition in a large, general purpose room.

Behavioral Context

Branch Manager—In-office detail and information flow demanded almost all of the branch manager's time. Such activity required him to spend half his time interacting with individual agents and all but a quarter of his time with the rest of his staff. He felt important and peerless in the branch.

The Agents—Normally, more than 75 percent of agent time was spent in prospecting, selling, collecting, and servicing outside the office. Agents usually barred first-line supervisors from their social cliques and directly sought out the branch manager very frequently. Agents had strong expectations that the first-line supervisor would help them with their selling activities, and yet they seldom viewed the first-line supervisor as a true supervisor. Some recent company policies threatened the deep sense of loyalty the agents felt for the company.

Obviously, these variables are not equally important determinants of assistant manager behavior, nor do they affect his behav or in the same way. Someone seeking to influence assistant manage behavior by manipulation of these determinants would certainly see some variables as more controllable, in the short run at least, than others. Interviews with the consultant showed that the researcher and consultant shared a simple descriptive model of the relative characteristics of the field of forces molding assistant manager behavior. The environmental variables seemed relatively unimportant, affected assistant manager behavior only indirectly, and were not easily controllable in the short run. On the other hand, both the structural and behavioral variables seemed quite important and seemed to affect assistant manager behavior rather directly. In this simple descriptive model these two sets of variables did not seem to differ significantly in importance or directness of influence. They did, however, differ in the degree of control that might be exercised over each. The structural variables seemed far more controllable than the behavioral variables. By way of summary, Exhibit 4–11 shows the

EXHIBIT 4–11
Descriptive Model Showing the Relative Importance,
Directness, and Controllability of the Three Sets of Variables
Molding Assistant Manager Behavior: Environmental
(E), Structural (S), and Behavioral (B)

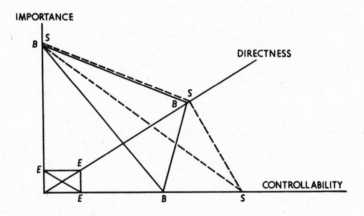

relative characteristics of the three sets of variables discussed in this chapter. Visualize the three sets of variables as simultaneously falling somewhere along each of three continua: important-unimportant, direct-indirect, controllable-uncontrollable. These three continua describe a three-dimensional field.

The next chapter details how the consultant wanted the first-line supervisor to behave and the way the consultant planned to alter the field of forces described above to achieve this behavioral change among first-line supervisors.

CHAPTER FIVE

Proposed Behavior Pattern and Plans to Effect the Change

INTRODUCTION

AFTER EXPLAINING the background of the consulting assignment, this chapter outlines the new behavior pattern proposed for the assistant manager (to replace the pattern described in Chapter Three) and the consultant's plans for achieving this change in behavior pattern. The first section, on the background of the consulting assignment, covers the stimulus for calling in the consultant, the mandate agreed upon for the consultant, and the events leading up to the consulting report. In the next section of this chapter the proposed behavior pattern is described in the same terms employed in describing the preconversion behavior in Chapter Three—the activities, interactions, and sentiments model. Finally, in his plans to achieve the behavior change, the consultant will be seen to "engineer" some of the forces spoken of in Chapter Four as influencing assistant manager behavior.

BACKGROUND OF THE CLIENT-CONSULTANT RELATIONSHIP

Before proceeding with the results of the consulting study a word is needed here about the background of the client-consultant relationship. In early 1960, the insurance company formed a top-level committee led by one of the staff vice presidents of the field sales division to study branch management compensation. The stimulus for this action was a concern of the senior vice president and other executives, particularly over the level of assistant manager income and turnover in this position. Also, the agent compensation plan had just been revised, so attention was drawn to the compensation arrangements for others within branches. Late that same year, the senior vice president, in search of a more effective approach than the internal committee, began exploratory talks with a director of one of the largest management consulting firms. Very early in these talks the consultants sensed that the branch management compensation issue was symptomatic of more fundamental problems. A number of the company executives also began to question whether adjusting branch organization and/or changing assistant manager compensation arrangements would remedy the worsening competitive position of the company. After performing a brief analysis of the competitive sales performance of the company, the consultants, toward the end of March 1961, submitted a proposal to work with the insurance company on the following:

1. Evaluating and strengthening the role played by your Branch Manager and Assistant Managers—including the ways in which they are compensated.

2. Making a more fundamental determination of (1) whether improvements in this particular area are the total answer to the basic problem you are seeking to solve and (2) what other specific improvement opportunities or needs, if any, you ought to capitalize on.

The consultants proposed as a first step "a diagnosis aimed at identifying and getting agreement on the basic reason or reasons for the decline in sales volume, in share-of-industry position, and in performance relative to your principal competitor." The proposal continued:

Although our experience shows that the kind of over-all diagnosis suggested above is important in gaining perspective and targeting subsequent improvement efforts, we would want—at the same time—to tie our early work as closely and quickly as possible into your immediate objective of strengthening your branch office plan of organization and branch management compensation.

In light of these two objectives, we would suggest that you think of our work with you as being divided into the following two phases:

Phase I: This phase would cover the over-all diagnosis already outlined, plus our recommendations on the area of your immediate interest. Specifically, the end products of this phase would be:

a. Our detailed recommendations on the plan of organization for personal-insurance field selling activities and on the way in which branch management personnel should be compensated.
b. The findings and conclusions from our over-all diagnosis on what other significant opportunities exist, if any, to further strengthen your marketing operations. As part of this step, of course, we would spell out a specific program for tackling each of these opportunities on a project basis.

Phase II: This phase would also consist of two parts. There would be:
a. Working with your personnel in implementing the agreed-upon recommendations covering branch office organization and compensation.
   Our experience shows that some follow-through of this kind on our part is clearly in the client's interest. One reason for this is that we can help build up and maintain momentum in the adoption of recommendations that have been agreed to in principle. Another is that some continuing contact on our part is usually necessary (1) to ensure full understanding by the individuals who will have a responsibility for making the recommendations work on a day-to-day basis and (2) to ensure that the anticipated benefits of the recommended changes are, in fact, realized.
b. Making a definitive study leading up to the development of specific recommendations on the *other* improvement areas that were identified through the diagnosis carried out in Phase I and that we all agree are important to recouping your sales position. Whether or not any added work of this sort would be in your interest would depend, of course, on the outcome of our diagnosis. In any event, this is something that we would all consider and reach full agreement on at that time.

The insurance company accepted the proposal, and the study began in June 1961. Eight home-office vice presidents were interviewed in depth as were eight territory supervisors and about a dozen other home office executives, almost all of whom held positions in the field sales division. The consultants attended—and read the previous minutes of—the Branch Management Compensation Committee meetings. They also reviewed internal sales reports and studies and analyzed company and industry data. During July and August the consultants spent two days in each of a sample of 22 branch offices across the country. In the course of these visits the consultants spent time with branch managers, assistant managers, and agents, observing and interviewing at length. (See Appendix I for the letter introducing the consulting firm to the branch offices.) By late August the diagnostic phase was producing patterns in critical areas, and the consulting team met to prepare for "working sessions" with the senior vice president. Oral feedback of findings and the gathering of supplementary and support data occupied most of September and early October.[1] By November the consultants were ready to make a formal presentation of findings coupled with general recommendations. This oral and graphic report was given to the senior vice president, then to small groups of staff vice presidents, and finally to the chief executive officer in early 1962. (See Appendix II for a topical outline of the material presented at that time.) This report completed Phase I as spelled out in the proposal.

By February 1962, top management of the insurance company agreed to Phase II of the consulting relationship. The recommendations approved in principle were translated into specific programs by mid-May so that the changes could be pilot tested in three branches. In July, it was decided to expand the pilot test to six more branches as of October. The consultants played the chief role in the conversion of the first three offices, then a lesser role in the next six. During the test, procedure manuals were written and forms were designed. In moving from the pilot tests to implementation on a national scale, a coincidence helped substantially. The branch managers' triennial national convention was scheduled for March 1963. The consultants chose this opportunity to "sell" the changes throughout the country by a program designed to expose the branch managers to the consultants' findings and to the recommended changes through testimonials from those who had already experienced them. It was at this meeting that the top management of the company made a public commitment to the national implementation of the recommended changes. In April, thirteen more branches were converted and a national conversion schedule was established. (See Appendix III for a timetable of events in the consultant-client relationship.)

With the above background we can now indicate what behavior pattern the consultants proposed for the assistant manager, then

---

[1]An important event occurred in October that was independent of the consultant's study (but which the consultants approved of) and yet closely related. As a result of a suggestion made by the senior vice president before the consultant's arrival, the organization structure was changed by inserting regional managers between the territory supervisor and the branch managers (see Exhibit 4–2). The change was made in part of only one territory in October but was proposed for the whole country. Ideally, each regional manager would have a span of control of about twenty branches, and a reduced number of territory supervisors would have a span of control of about six regional managers.

move on to how specifically this change was to be effected. First, it must be clear that one of the changes has narrowed our population of assistant managers to three quarters of its size in 1961. The consultants proposed distinguishing between assistant managers who supervised regular agents and those who supervised special agents. The research focus narrows to cover only those who supervise regular agents—*Regular managers.* The proposed behavior pattern here expressed in terms of activities, interactions, and sentiments is drawn primarily from the formal guide given to the regular manager at conversion time, from the report of findings and recommendations outlined in Appendix II, from memoranda of the consulting team, and from statements of intent given in interviews by the consultants and the top company management.

PROPOSED BEHAVIOR PATTERN FOR REGULAR MANAGERS

Activities

In a normal workweek the regular manager would spend about 35 percent of his time on in-office activities. An individual conference with each of his agents would consume about an hour for each man. Depending on the varying needs of the agent, the conference could run from 15 minutes to well over an hour. This unpredictability required the regular manager to schedule an hour for each man. The conference itself had no set format, but the time was to be spent in a dialogue concerned with planning the next week's activities and a follow-up or control check on last week's activities. Specific preparation for each of these conferences, including midweek supervisory or follow-up phone calls and a diagnostic review of the agent's performance, could require about 15 minutes a week per agent. The regular manager would spend another hour each week conducting a unit (new title of the group of agents assigned each regular manager) conference in which he would first communicate home office directives and announcements, then lead the group in a participative educational experience, weaving in appropriate recognition and motivation. Preparation for such a conference could consume one to two hours weekly—previewing film strips, studying directives and policy changes, priming agents for making a contribution to the meeting, and so forth. Another hour each week would be dedicated to an individual conference with the branch manager in which there was to be a planning and controlling dialogue. Specific preparation for this conference should be minimal after the regular manager had completed his weekly record keeping and reporting processing and report-making activities. These latter activities would probably occupy the regular manager for about two hours a week. Like the preparation time for agent conferences and unit conferences, these paper-flow functions—in some cases necessarily—would be done in not one but several sittings. Later—in the information flow section—specifics will be presented. Here, it suffices to indicate that the regular manager is involved in information flow as follows:

Weekly:—initiates one control report
　　　　—receives and processes two control reports and one planning form
　　　　—updates two control records*
Monthly:—receives and processes four control reports*
　　　　—initiates one planning form
Quarterly:—initiates one planning form
Annually:—initiates two planning forms*
Periodically (some with more than daily frequency) :
　　　　—receives and processes two quasi-control forms and two procedural forms*

The balance of the regular manager's normal workweek time was to be spent in field or clinical training of individual agents. This activity should be distinguished from "demonstration selling"—a phrase invented early in this study to identify the practice of virtually selling for the agent. The objective of the proposed activity was not so much to put business on the books now as it was to make the agent self-reliant for future sales.

Nonprogrammed activities still would consume the regular manager's time in rather an unpredictable fashion. A nonprogrammed but continuing activity would be recruiting in anticipation of need, not only to satisfy a current need. The regular manager would collect and service only those agencies vacant, because of termination or disability, in his unit. Also, he could still anticipate taking his turn in teaching the career extension course for new agents every 18 months or so (two hours a week for six months). Periodically the regular manager might contribute his expertise in a particular area at another unit's meeting or to all the agents in the branch at a

---

*Signifies multiple forms of documents relating to each agent—hence multiply by a factor of seven or eight.

special session. In emergency cases only the regular manager would assist a brother regular manager service an open agency. No longer would the regular manager have to spend two weeks every 18 months with each agent auditing his accounts. Home-office auditors assumed this function.

EXHIBIT 5–1
Percent of Regular Manager Normal Workweek
to Be Spent in Various Activities

Field and clinical training 65
Individual agent conferences 17*
Unit conference 3
Conference with branch manager 3
Conference preparation 7
Records and reports 5

*This would vary with the number of agents on the unit. A seven-man unit was assumed here.

Interactions

About 85 percent of the regular manager's time should be spent with his agents: about 2½ percent in a group context. If the unit was composed of seven agents, about 17½ percent of the workweek would be consumed in individual, across-the-desk, hour-long dialogues. In both the individual and group situations, the regular manager would initiate about 50 percent of the time—to encourage agent participation and contribution. The initiation pattern would change of necessity to more initiation on the part of the regular manager during the balance of time spent with individual agents in training sessions. Though no set policy was laid down, the regular manager might well distribute this 65 percent of his week to more than one agent, based on priority needs. In any event, it would no longer be feasible to have contact with an agent for the same long, extended periods possible under the former system where all of Monday, Tuesday PM, and all of Wednesday and Thursday were free for this type of interaction. Other programmed activities (especially the conferences) would cause some chopping up of these large blocks of time. The regular manager had one programmed, face-to-face contact with the branch manager. Being a dialogue, the initiations would be shared about equally. The branch manager weekly initiated one written contact and the regular manager initiated one in return. Interaction with the branch manager then occupied something more than 3 percent of the time. As part of the information flow system, the regular manager would have frequent but short oral and written contact—most as responder—with the clerks, amounting to possibly 2 percent of the workweek. The remaining 10 percent of the workweek was for noncontact activities, usually alone in the regular manager office.

EXHIBIT 5-2
Percent of Regular Manager Workweek to Be Spent
Interacting with Various People

With individual agents .... 82 (10.0) *
With group of agents 3   (1.5)
With branch manager alone 3   (1.5)
With clerks 2   (1.5)

*Figures in ( ) indicate percent initiated by other party.

Sentiments

Basically, the regular manager was to feel like a true member of management, responsible for the performance of each agent on his unit. He must have a balanced interest in putting quality business on the books and conserving appropriate insurance already in force. He must add, too, a longer-term view of the cultivation of manpower resources with potential and the development of market segments in line with new company marketing strategies. Commitment to unit performance should leave room for branch spirit, particularly management team spirit. Finally, he should look upon his as a position worthy to be a career position with the company.

BASIC CONVERSION POLICIES

Before, and at the beginning of Phase II of the consulting relationship, client and consultant agreed on a series of basic conversion policies. First, the new system—referred to as the Line Management System—was to be pilot tested. The consultants would be the primary change agents in these pilot branches where the system would be "debugged" and the conversion techniques would be polished. Observing the first three conversions and assuming the chief change-agent role in the next six would be company executives, one in particular, who would guide the nationwide conversion process. Also involved were the regional managers (conversion was begun in the territory where regional managers were first appointed in October 1961). As later branches were converted, the responsible regional manager would become the chief change agent, with the home office guidance of the company conversion coordinator. The second major policy, then, was that the system would be installed by the line officer of the company on the scene—assisted by one temporary staff assistant—with the home-office advice from a vice president in the temporary staff position of the conversion coordinator. Transitionally, the consultant would give field assistance to new regional managers on their first conversion but would phase out as soon as the conversion coordinator had arranged for an adequate home-office training program for new regional managers. Other than this early participation, the consultant would be available for policy conferences with home-office executives.

A third basic policy stated that the new system would be installed full blown in each branch. The changes would not be phased in. Also, detailed official communication about the changes would be distributed to each branch only when its turn for conversion came. A fourth related policy was that, after an initial bellwether branch conversion in each region, four branches per region per quarter would be converted. Regional managers would begin their 18-month to two-year conversion process as soon as they had been assigned and adequately trained. From the first pilot test branch to the last branch converted, the process would take about four years.

The fifth policy was another critical timing issue. Consultant and client decided to go ahead with the conversions without any formal off-the-job training for the branch managers or regular managers. Formal programs were in preparation but would be ready only after over a hundred offices were scheduled for conversion. Reliance was placed on an orientation period of four days for the branch managers and two days for the regular managers just prior to the branch conversion. The regional manager and his assistant would conduct a discussion of written "Guides," distributed just prior to conversion, which explained the changes and the reasons for the changes, and suggested some "patterns" of managerial performance. The branch management team also received about five days of explanation of, and supervised work with, the mechanics of the new branch marketing plan. With the help of the written "Guides," branch management gained competence by a two-level, supervised learning-by-doing process. The regional manager was to supervise the branch manager's learning by doing, and the branch manager was to supervise the regular manager's learning by doing. This policy turned out to be twofold: (1) a preconversion information and exhortation program[2] and (2) a postconversion supervised learning-by-doing program. No specific plan was made as of April 1963 for the utilization, prior to conversion, of the formal training programs being developed for branch and regular managers.[3]

RATIONAL PLANS RELATING TO BASIC INFLUENCES ON REGULAR MANAGER BEHAVIOR

Chapter Four outlined the forces that molded regular manager behavior as of the beginning of 1961. The consultants engineered some of those forces in order to change regular manager behavior to conform to the pattern drawn earlier in this chapter. Other than the information and exhortation program and the supervised learning-by-doing program described immediately above, these engineered influences are the independent variables used in effecting the change in behavior pattern. It should be clear that the consultant was attempting to change a whole system. Therefore, some of the alteration of the basic influences was designed to produce changes in areas other than the regular manager's behavior pattern. While the change in regular manager behavior is not the only proposed change (refer again to the outline of the consultant's findings and general recommendations in Appendix II), the researcher judged that change in regular manager behavior would be a clear index of change in the rest of the system. Given this judgment about the regular manager behavior, the section below relates the consultant's plans—in terms of the basic influences as outlined in Chapter Four—to the change they were to effect.

Little Is Done with Environmental Context

It has been pointed out already that the elements of the environmental context—the buyer's and seller's sides of the market; institutional arrangements like government regulation, trade and professional associations, and unions; financial, technological, and man-

---

[2]This program was observed in full by the researcher when branches 7 and 8 were converted.

[3]Client and consultant reasoned that preconversion training might well be so distracting that preconversion branch productivity would be seriously hurt.

power resources—are virtually uncontrollable in the short run even for a company the size of the one in question here. These factors affect regular manager behavior rather indirectly and in a less significant way than some of the other influences treated below. The external economic variables were taken as givens—as constraints. State regulation on allowable expenses set some parameters of what could be done with compensation. Certain union contract[4] clauses limited how the schedule could be changed in branch offices. In the realm of internal economics one significant move was made when the same consulting firm was engaged to direct a clerical cost-reduction program in branch offices. This study, conducted independently of the one analyzed here, began about a year after the first. The effort streamlined clerical systems and procedures and introduced the first piece of automated equipment into branch offices for the processing of policyholder payments. These improvements allowed for a clerical reduction in many areas of a third or more—the reduction was to be achieved by normal attrition. The net effect was the promise of a loosening of the constraint of out-of-line costs. Direct impact on regular manager behavior was not intended. In the manpower area no dramatic changes were planned. In general, the new system was to be administered by the management personnel already in office in each branch. One small but important effort was begun early in the consulting engagement. The company began to hire the nucleus of a cadre of young men with Master of Business Administration degrees to upgrade managerial talent in an accelerated program. One other move was made in the manpower area—this by specific consultant recommedation. In the future the bulk of special agents was to be hired directly from outside the company rather than promoted from the ranks of the regular agents.

A specific point is made here of covering the elements of the environmental context despite the fact that the consultant did not—and could not in the short run—plan to engineer them to effect changes in regular manager behavior. Historically, studies of this type, classified often as "plant sociology," have been accused of ignoring independent variables tangential to the narrowly defined system being analyzed. In this case the environmental context was considered and no change took place—planned or otherwise—to facilitate or retard

---

[4] In anticipation of union contract negotiation in the fall of 1963, the company did make a special effort through the company newspaper and other channels to keep the union informed of the character of the changes.

the change in regular manager behavior other than those noted above.

Systemic Alterations Were the Most Important

The consultant planned detailed modifications in the structural context surrounding the regular manager. Virtually all of the formal design was engineered, not as an end in itself but rather as a means effecting a behavioral change leading to more efficient utilization of management resources in achieving the fundamental goals of the company.

Authority Structure. Above the branch level the personal life field sales division was restructured (see Exhibit 5–3). Compare with the 1961 structure shown in Exhibit 4–2. The truly significant change here was the extension of the regional manager concept already internally developed and tried in a pilot test in October 1961. Formal guides, written for every position from senior vice president to regular manager, specified in sophisticated job description form the shift from procedural control, largely dictated by home-office staff, to end result control administered by the scalar chain of line

EXHIBIT 5–3
Restructured Personal Life Sales Division Organization Chart

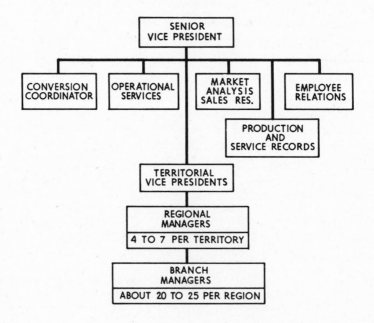

management. Authority and accountability for results were specified for each level. The following excerpt from the *Regional Manager's Guide* spells out his responsibility:

The Regional Manager is accountable for *both* short-term and long-term improvement in the end result achievement of the branches in his region. His performance, thus, will be measured each year on: (a) the amount (business measured by the New Performance Measure) his region achieves in relation to the potential of the area and (b) the extent to which he has built increasingly capable Branch Managers—this being the best measure of how well he has fulfilled his responsibilities for ensuring the long-term growth of the company in his region.

Another passage from this 100-page guide captures the spirit of the change and indicates the character of the relationship with the branch manager:

1. *Direct personal contact with Branch Managers:* The Regional Manager will train and supervise almost exclusively through direct personal contact rather than through correspondence and third-party communication. It is expected that he will spend at least two-thirds of his time in the branches of his region, working directly with Branch Managers. This close and continuing contact should lead to an intimate—and candid—relationship between the Regional Manager and Branch Manager, based on mutual respect for each other's responsibilities and capabilities. Once such a relationship has developed, there is little danger or reason for concern that the Regional Manager might infringe on the Branch Manager's authority or try to "run his branch for him." At the same time, the Regional Manager will be responsible for evaluating and appraising the Branch Manager's accomplishments and taking or recommending appropriate action where results are unsatisfactory.

2. *Individualized and selective management:* The Regional Manager is expected to concentrate on working with Branch Managers on an individual basis helping them to solve existing problems to bring about short-term improvements in results; and helping them develop the capacity to solve future problems as they arise—thereby building long-term strength into local management. Such individualized attention will not be distributed equally among the Managers of his region, however, because Branch Managers obviously vary in their needs for training and guidance. In short, the Regional Manager's approach will be one of selective management, as opposed to group or mass management.

Within the branch, the consultants planned alterations in authority structure that extended the same kind of clearly defined line responsibility—a form of decentralization in effect (compare Exhibit 5–4 with the organization chart in Exhibit 4–3).

Passages in the *Branch Manager's Guide* show that the branch has been raised to the status of a mutual insurance company's counterpart of a profit center:

The Branch Manager is the key Management figure in the Line Management System of organization. The company centers its local responsibility and authority in his position. . . .

Since the Branch Manager retains the responsibilities described previously for his position, these are briefly reviewed:

1. Develop and maintain a sales program
2. Recruit and select branch personnel
3. Train and develop branch personnel
4. Motivate branch personnel
5. Administer office detail, and
6. Develop and maintain good public relations

In addition to these basic responsibilities, the Branch Manager assumes two additional ones under the Line Management System. These are to:

(a) plan and direct the long-term program of the branch, and

(b) exercise direct control over branch expenses.

Both of these are significant responsibilities which have been previously reserved for higher levels of management. Thus, their delegation to the Branch Manager significantly enlarges his scope of responsibility.

The Branch Manager will carry out his responsibilities in a different manner under the Line Management System. Instead of dealing directly

EXHIBIT 5–4
Restructured Branch Office Organization Chart

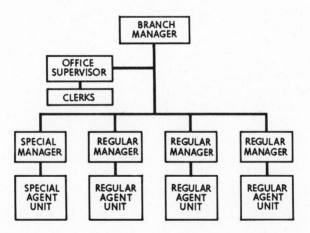

with each member of the branch, he will delegate individual supervision on a controlled basis to his Regular and Special Managers. This delegation does not relieve him of the responsibility for the end result, but it does require different methods for the successful direction of his branch's activities.

Since these changes in method necessitate a reorientation of Branch Managers to their assignments, a series of patterns has been developed to provide guidelines in operating under the new organizational structure. . . .

The "patterns" spoken of tell the branch manager how to go about his job on a day-to-day basis—guides based more on fundamental managerial principles than on procedures. The patterns fill 27 pages of the *Branch Manager's Guide* under the following headings:

1. Managing a branch during the first six months of Line Management operation.
2. Directing the regular activities of the branch.
3. Determining which units warrant priority attention from the Branch Manager.
4. Diagnosing in depth a unit's problems and opportunities.
5. Planning and scheduling the time to be spent with each unit.
6. Working with Regular and Special Managers to develop improvement plans.
7. Following through to achieve the desired end results.
8. Evaluating Regular and Special Manager performance.
9. Maintaining performance records.

In pattern six the nature of the branch reorganization becomes clear in the changed relationship between branch manager and regular manager:

This relationship should be on a first name basis if the discussion is to be full and frank. Unless the Regular Manager can feel at ease in talking with the Branch Manager, the chances of his telling the Branch Manager both the worst and best aspects of his unit's operation are very remote.

Accountability for the plans or courses of action developed must always rest, in the end, with the Regular Manager: The Branch Manager's job is to develop Regular Managers who can produce the end results that he specifies. If the Branch Manager "orders" the course of action, this relieves the Regular Manager of end-result accountability if the plan should fail. For example, the Branch Manager has weakened his position of managerial leadership if a Regular Manager reports back that, "We followed your instructions, but the plan didn't work. What do you want us to do next?"

This does not mean that the Branch Manager must simply listen and accept whatever is proposed by his Regular Managers. He should feel free to counsel and offer guidance as to methods for achieving the desired end results. He should usually suggest several approaches to keep from being personally identified with any single solution. And, of course, if the Branch Manager is effective in building the proper relationship with his Regular Managers, any of his ideas and approaches will be welcomed by them and, often, incorporated into their final plans. Nevertheless, in the end, the Regular Manager must decide on the specific action plan that he considers best to achieve his unit's objective. When this is done, the Regular Manager makes a commitment for which he can be held accountable. In these situations, the Branch Manager is then left in the position, if the plan does not produce the desired end results, to say, "Your program did not work. What do you propose to do about it?"

The change in the branch manager's role in the authority structure is almost sufficient commentary in itself on the drastically altered role of the regular manager. He is no longer to be a staff assistant exercising *ad hoc* functional authority over any one of the agents specified by the branch manager, as is clear from this paragraph from the *Regular Manager's Guide:*

The Line Management System will require a major change in the job perspective of Regular Managers. The men in these assignments will no longer be technical specialists in selling. Nor will their performance be measured primarily by their personal production during assignment weeks. Instead, Regular Managers will have line responsibility for the accumulated results every week, of a unit usually composed of seven to ten men. . . . The Regular Managers become directly accountable for the end results of their individual units under the Line Management System of organization. Thus the company centers major responsibility in their positions as its first level of management authority.

The new role is detailed as follows:

In this position of line authority, the Regular Managers will be directly responsible for the following activities:

1. Prepare the Individual Action Plans Necessary to Accomplish the Unit's End-Result Objectives: Acceptable results come from sound planning and careful follow through. Regular Managers will ensure the development of adequate plans for agents and the preparation of an over-all unit action program which will produce the required results. Branch Managers will review these detailed plans of Regular Managers to assure themselves that unit as well as branch objectives will be achieved.

2. Supervise the Regular Activities of Agents: As a prime responsibility

of Regular Managers, this managerial role extends beyond the former report-taking procedure. It becomes, in fact, the joint agreement between Regular Managers and their men on the productive use of time. The portion of this individualized supervision which has previously been handled by the Branch Manager should be assumed by the Regular Managers.

3. Schedule Training Assignments: Although the Regular Managers will seek the Branch Manager's guidance in scheduling training assignments, this will be primarily the responsibility of the Regular Managers. The time required to plan and carry out these training assignments will be a major part of the investment they make in their work with individual agents.

4. Building Agents to Become Skilled, Self-Reliant Field Representatives: Since the Regular Manager cannot succeed alone by his personal production efforts on assignments, he must assume a longer term attitude toward training and manpower development. He must build the selling skills of his men rather than simply sell for them. Thus he will check closely their production during the weeks following training assignments. The production momentum carried forward from assignments will serve as his reward for his earlier investment of time.

The regular Manager's desire to increase earnings by enlarging his unit's productive manpower can be achieved by reducing turnover and by developing self-reliant, successful agents.

5. Motivating Individual Agents to Reach Higher Levels of Accomplishment: Since his success is so directly linked with that of his agents, the Regular Manager must become the personal counselor of his men. Instead of mass stimulation, he can employ the more reliable man-to-man approach for discussions, encouragement, sight setting, and follow-up. This personal interest should reassure agents that they are not just members of a branch audience, but are individuals whose personal problems and success are of utmost concern to a particular member of branch management.

6. Recruiting and Selecting Superior Candidates: The Regular Managers' greatest investment of time will come during the introduction and initial training of new agents. To reduce the number of unnecessary or unproductive introductions, the Regular Managers must recruit and select the best men available. Their success in this activity will directly influence not only their immediate compensation but their later earnings potential.

7. Ensuring Quality Service for Policyholders and Prospects: This plan should provide a greater continuity of management attention to policyholders. Since the Regular Manager cannot move away from his policyholders following an assignment, he will be more interested in the quality of their service all along. This quality will be reflected in a reduction in time wasted in performing routine administration and the receipt of premium payments and increased income from receptive prospects for additional insurance purchases and referrals.

Line responsibility makes each Regular Manager accountable for determining the use of his personal time. His record will be the combined record of his agency unit. On this record his performance will be evaluated, he will be recognized, and he will be compensated.

Although the primary emphasis for the Regular Manager will be encountered upon his agency unit, he will retain certain branch responsibilities as a part of the branch management team.

"Patterns" are offered the regular manager, too, as guides to his everyday operations. In a 21-page section of the *Regular Manager's Guide* these patterns appear under headings similar (with obviously appropriate changes) to the *Branch Manager's Guide* except for the last three.

    8. Planning and conducting a unit meeting.
    9. Recruiting and selecting agents.
    10. Maintaining performance records.

Organizationally, the regular and special managers, though now with different assignments, remain organizational peers.

Do not allow reference to the "guides" and official organization charts to confuse our reason for presenting the new authority system here. The use of "guides" as part of the planned information and exhortation conversion effort has been explained earlier in this chapter. The new organization structure is presented here to indicate part of the planned systemic alterations aimed at producing behavioral changes. *The very fact that the formal design of the organization has been officially changed affects behavior.* The change may be slight and only attitudinal, but it is a first step. The regular manager at least knew that in design or on paper his world was very different.

Reward Structure. The fundamental systemic alteration in the area of rewards deals with the new performance measure that affected compensation, recognition, and promotion. As pointed out earlier, the basis for rewards had been performance against company average on a number of subjectively weighted factors. Heavy emphasis was placed on the *volume* of business in force and the *volume* of net first-year commissions earned. The innovation targeted attention on the variables most meaningful in terms of the company objectives. In a single measure it includes *(a)* new premiums (annualized premium on policies sold this year), *(b)* premiums lost through policy lapse (annualized premium on policies sold in this or previous years but now dropped by the policyholder), and (c) a variable and fixed expense standard. The New Performance Measure (NPM) was used in two forms: NPM $1 = a - b$; NPM $2 = a - b - \$$ over c. How this performance measure entered into the newly devised planning and control system will be covered below under "Information-Flow System."

The regular manager's new compensation formula contained the following elements: a nationally standardized fixed base somewhat smaller than he previously had as a minimum base, unit incentive compensation figured as a percent of NPM 1 generated by the agents on his unit, and branch incentive compensation determined as a percent of the pool of NPM 2 generated by all the agents in the branch, divided equally among the regular and special managers in the branch. A typical management compensation might be 40 percent fixed base, 45 percent unit incentive compensation, and 15 percent branch incentive compensation. Policy still allowed the regular manager to supplement his income by earning commissions on personally written business. Special policies compensated the regular manager for losing an agent and/or agency through transfer or promotion, for assuming a development unit (one with expansion potential but too small initially to support a regular manager), and for emergency situations like regional economic recession. Transitional arrangements protected a regular manager for a year from being adversely affected by the compensation changes. No new length-of-service differentials would be offered, but those already earned would remain. Incidentially, special managers were paid on an analogous basis, except that they received a 25 percent differential in fixed salary. The branch manager, too, had a fixed base—now standardized nationally—and incentive compensation figured as a percentage of NPM 2 generated by the whole branch. He also received an annual bonus based on percent of NPM 2 objective achieved and the relative size of the objective. The agent still operated on the same compensation contract—service and renewal commissions on business in force, net first-year commissions, and a conservation payment based on performance relative to company average.[5]

Recognition through sales trophy standing ceased to exist. Branch-

---

[5] The agent's contract was changed after the field work was completed on this study. Most importantly, the conservation payment was replaced by a payment figured as a percent of NPM 1 generated by the agent.

to-branch comparisons were to be made on the basis of percent of NPM 2 objective achieved; units were to be ranked by percent of NPM 1 objective achieved. The Distinction Club remained and agents qualified as before, but regular managers no longer qualified as a group if a certain percent of the branch's agents qualified or if the branch enjoyed a certain national or territorial standing in the sales trophy. Now each regular manager qualified if his unit achieved a certain minimum percent of the NPM 1 or if a certain percent of his agents qualified. It was optional at the regional and branch level if recognition bulletins were to be published.

No formal changes were made in promotion policy, but the understanding was general that regular managers would be promoted directly to branch manager status rather than indirectly through sales education or territory supervisor's staff. Clearly, the regular manager position as newly constituted provided a realistic training ground for branch managers, and the New Performance Measure added an objective criterion for selecting men for promotion.

Work-Flow System and Schedule. The consultant made no change in the fundamental work-flow system in which the agent was primarily involved and the regular manager was secondarily involved —prospecting, selling, collecting, and servicing. In the old Tuesday-Friday report and deposit schedule, the regular manager was involved in his check-off function. Twice a week he checked each agent's report, deposit, and lapse control before the agent submitted his report and turned in his collections. This check-off function no longer delayed the agent in finishing his business with the clerk at the deposit window. The agent still deposited twice a week but on a staggered schedule that had only one unit of agents in the office at a time. Contact with the regular manager was scheduled for a one-hour individual conference once a week, usually on a deposit day. In the new system the regular manager did not have a function—was not a necessary station—in the agent's weekly in-office work flow. In the weekly conference, the elements of the check-off were covered but outside of the work flow incident to deposit. The weekly conference, however, very much involved the regular manager in the agent's extra-office work flow of prospecting and selling. The agent's week began at this conference, and plans were made for the next week's prospecting and selling. Also, plans for last week's prospecting and selling were checked for results. The schedule was modified, too, so that a weekly unit conference replaced the general meeting usually held on Friday morning. Finally, a weekly scheduled, individual conference with the branch manager replaced the group management meeting usually held on Thursday afternoon. Under the new workflow system a regular manager's typical schedule would be as shown in Exhibit 5–5.

EXHIBIT 5–5
Typical Regular Manager's In-Office Schedule

	Monday	Tuesday	Wednesday	Thursday	Friday
8 A.M.			Agent conference		
9 A.M.		Unit conference			
10 A.M.		Agent conference	Branch mgr. conference		
11 A.M.		Agent conference		Agent conference	
1 P.M.				Agent conference	
2 P.M.				Agent conference	
3 P.M.				Agent conference	
4 P.M.					

Information-Flow System. The new Branch Marketing Plan made the regular manager a critical figure in the sending, receiving, processing, and storing of information. For all practical purposes he formerly stood outside the relatively unsophisticated planning and controlling information flow—not so in the new system (see Exhibit 5–6).

In addition to the regular manager's involvement in the planning and control process, he is frequently a processor in the paper flow concerning transfers (a policy from one agent to another) and exemptions (requests for relief from responsibility for a particular policyholder's insurance). Often messages from clerks may acquaint him with situations where policyholder service calls have not been tended by his agents or home-office correspondence from particular agents is tardy or incomplete. Monthly, he processes reports from

EXHIBIT 5–6.   Proposed Information Flow Involving the Regular Manager

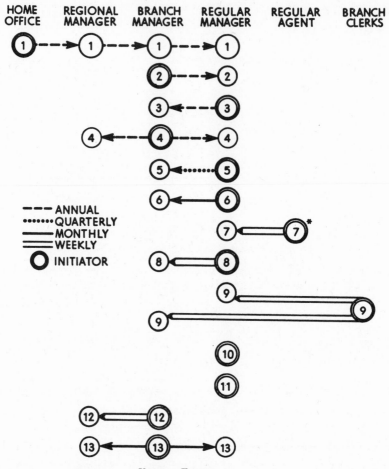

HOME OFFICE	REGIONAL MANAGER	BRANCH MANAGER	REGULAR MANAGER	REGULAR AGENT	BRANCH CLERKS

--- ANNUAL
······ QUARTERLY
—— MONTHLY
═══ WEEKLY
○ INITIATOR

KEY TO FIGURE

1. Guidelines→marketing support plans.

2. Branch planning guidelines (market potential, human and financial resources).

3. Determination of N. P. M. 1. attainable from assigned agents and requirements on Regular Manager's time to achieve same (twofold process: (a) determining potential of each agent—form for each agent; and (b) setting unit objectives.) Reworked until Branch Manager's approval is received.

4. Determination of branch N. P. M. 2. objectives, also manpower and growth objectives. Reworked until Regional Manager's approval is received.

5. Quarterly objectives, time usage, and recruiting plans. Reworked until Branch Manager's approval is received.

6. Monthly work plan of day-to-day activities.

7. Weekly plan for prospecting and selling.

8. Weekly report of "writings" by agents in unit.

9. Weekly report of "placings" and lapses by agents in unit.

10. Weekly record of progress in N. P. M. 1.

11. Weekly updating of analytic record of agent performance.

12. Weekly report of "writings" of units in branch.

13. Monthly report of progress in N. P. M. 1. by units in branch.

°Used at the option of the regular manager.

the clerks concerning the state of each agent's book of accounts. Finally, through the branch manager, the regular manager weekly receives communications from the home office relative to product-line changes, procedural changes, advertising and sales promotion campaigns, new sales aids, contests, and such, which he in turn is to communicate to the agents in his unit.

Physical Structure. In moving from branch to unit as the basic work group in each office and in adjusting the schedule of deposit days and individual and unit conferences, the office layout pictured in Exhibit 4–6 was inadequate. The economic constraint dictated the utilization of the same square footage in a more appropriate layout. Exhibit 5–7 pictures a typical remodeling of a branch office (the same office that appeared in Exhibit 4–6). The change was standardized nationally, with physical conversion to coincide with conversion to line management. Note the following basic physical changes. The regular managers now have private offices instead of desks in the regular agents' room. The regular agents now have individual file space instead of the desks in the large regular agents' room. The agents' work area is reduced to one third the size of the former area. Agents whose units were not scheduled for deposit could utilize the large table in the work area and have access to their files, to the clerks' windows, and to their mailboxes. Another third of the former regular agents' room was converted into a professionally appointed conference room for unit conferences and for work space for agents whose units were scheduled for deposit. The special manager, too, has a private office, and his special agents have private or semiprivate offices. Note, finally, that space is provided for two clerical aides to service the special manager and his special agents.

Planned Alterations in the Behavioral Context

Since the regular manager did not behave in a vacuum, the behavior patterns of those around him had to be modified if his was to change. The interdependence of the branch office operation demanded this. The sheer logic of the shift to the new system would seem to dictate that some of the alterations in the regular manager's behavioral context would precede the changes in his own behavior— if not in a causal sequence then as an enabling or facilitating condition. This would certainly be true of certain phases of the branch manager's behavior for two reasons: First, part of the essence of the

EXHIBIT 5–7

Typical Branch Office Floor Plan after Conversion

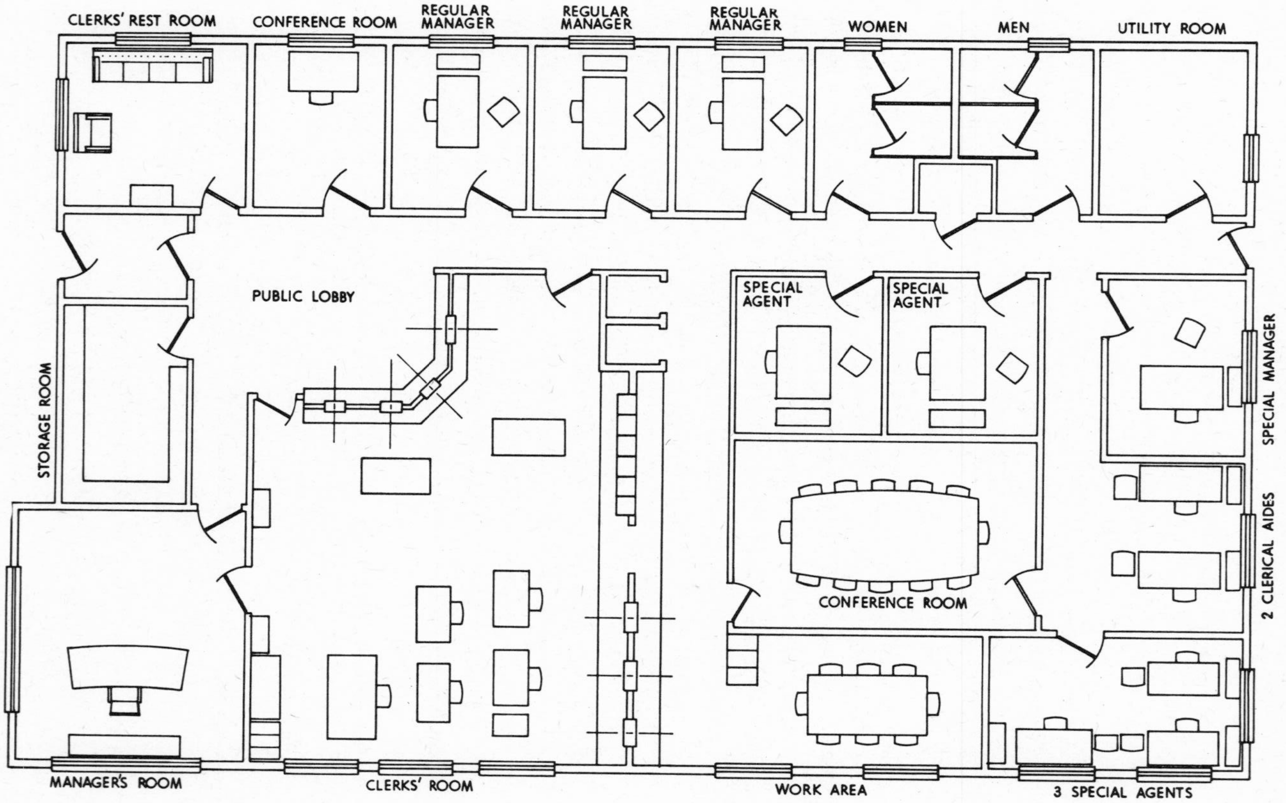

new system in the branch was decentralization, delegation from branch manager to regular manager. Second, consultant and client formulated as one of the basic conversion policies that regular manager behavior pattern change, in part, would be effected by supervised (by the branch manager) learning by doing.

Note that the behavioral context could not be engineered directly as was the structural context. Modifications in branch manager and agent behavior were to be effected by the same forces that were to change regular manager behavior—information and exhortation, supervised learning by doing, systemic alterations, and alterations in the behavioral context. The branch manager was subjected to one of these forces before the regular manager. All branch managers experienced a one-day information and exhortation effort in March 1963 at their triennial meeting. Also, the regional manager began the preconversion information and exhortation program for the branch manager two days before the regular manager's program. Below are some of the modifications in the behavioral context that could be viewed as part of the plans to effect the change in regular manager behavior or at least to facilitate or enable the change.

Branch Manager. The bulk of the branch manager's time should be managing his regular and special managers—training them in all phases of their jobs, assisting them in plan formulation, supervising them in plan accomplishment, and evaluating their performances against the plans. The only weekly programmed phase of this managing activity was the hour-long individual conference with each. The diagnostic preparation for this activity would consume much time in analysis of market and manpower potential, analysis of performance records, and probably even observation of the regular manager in action during unit conferences. Long-range planning, administration of clerical work, information processing, report making, record keeping, and the maintenance of policyholder and public relations would occupy the balance of his time.

The significant modification in interaction pattern for the branch manager would be the drastic curtailment of initiations and total time with the agents as individuals and as a group. In individual contacts with regular managers he would share the initiations so that the conference in truth would be a dialogue. Part of his programmed interactions were at least three sessions with the regional manager and/or the assistant regional manager in the first six months following conversion. Beyond that, interaction with the regional manager would be scheduled according to priorities set by the regional manager for all his branches.

In the area of sentiments, it was chiefly the branch manager's self-image that was to be altered. He should view himself as a manager of managers, a delegator who retained responsibility for the branch end results.

Regular Agent. Agent activities were more rescheduled than altered substantially in time allocation. He deposited twice a week without the "check-off" by the regular manager, and he attended a unit conference once a week. In addition, he allocated an hour for a conference with his regular manager. Only the last was a change in anything but the weekly schedule.

In interactions the agent was to behave quite differently. First, he would have considerably less contact with the branch manager individually and in a group. He would interact with the regular manager more in in-office situations (individual and unit conferences), where he would have the opportunity to share the initiations and offer his own contributions. The new schedule dictated, too, that "assignments" with the regular manager would be for shorter periods. The old two-week "assignment" in which the two were together almost continually each day would no longer exist. Incidentally, the agent's interaction pattern with his peers was changed in the new system. He no longer would be in the office with all the other agents at the same time (meetings of all the branch personnel would be annual or semiannual at most), as he was formerly on each Tuesday and Friday for deposit and for the Friday general meeting. In-office activity was now scheduled by unit (a work group he had no hand in choosing and could not alter).

The critical sentiment or attitude modification the agent had to make was the acceptance of the regular manager as his "boss" instead of the branch manager. He had to value the more personal attention afforded him in his individual conference and in the unit conference. He had to replace branch spirit with unit spirit.

SUMMARY

The consultant proposed a study project with two objectives: (1) to strengthen the branch office plan of organization and branch management and (2) to determine what significant opportunities exist to strengthen the company's marketing operations. The diagnostic phase of the study began in June 1961, and detailed recommendations were presented in the spring of 1962. A critical part of these recommendations was the proposed behavior pattern for the newly titled first-line supervisor, the regular manager.

The proposed behavior pattern differed from the behavior observed originally, especially in that the first-line supervisor was expected to change his chief activity from "demonstration selling" (putting business on the books for agents) to "field and clinical training" (preparing his agents to be self-reliant life underwriters). The other differences are evident in Exhibit 5–8.

EXHIBIT 5–8
Percent of First-Line Supervisor Normal Workweek
Spent in Various Activities

Generalized Observations before Conversion		*Pattern Proposed by Consultant*	
Demonstration selling	75	Field and clinical training	65
Conservation	5	Individual agent conferences	17
Processing agent reports	10	Unit conference	3
Group meetings	7–8	Conference with branch manager	3
Office detail	2–3	Conference preparation	7
		Records and reports	5

Such a proposed distribution of activity time did not ostensibly require drastic changes in the first-line supervisor's interaction pattern (see Exhibit 5–9). At root, the change was in the direction of initiation, in the sensitive balance of initiating and responding in contacts with agents and branch manager. The proposed pattern called for a dialogue between first-line supervisor and agent in individual conferences. The same dialogue was expected in unit conferences with his agents and in the individual conference with the branch manager. The dialogue pattern required the first-line super-

EXHIBIT 5–9
Percent of First-Line Supervisor Normal
Workweek Spent Interacting with Various People

	Generalized Observations before Conversion		*Pattern Proposed by Consultant*	
With individual agents	85	(2) *	82	(10.0)
With group of agents			3	(1.5)
With branch manager alone	1	(1)	3	(1.5)
With branch manager in group	7–8	(7–8)		
With clerks	1	(1)	2	(1.5)

* ( ) indicates percent initiated by other party.

visor to move away from his habit of dominance with his subordinates and from his "responder" role in contacts with his superior. One other noteworthy change is that the first-line supervisor is programmed to be alone for 5 percent more of his workweek.

The chief sentiment change would come in the first-line supervisor's self-image from supersalesman to supervisor, having responsibility for the development of his own unit of agents. His new stature would bring him to see his position as a career position, not merely a way station on route to the branch manager's chair.

In planning for this behavorial change, the consultant formulated five basic conversion policies:

1. The new system was to be pilot tested.
2. The consultant would phase out of the implementation of the system so that the responsible line officers of the company would administer the conversion process.
3. The whole new system would be installed at once in each branch as its turn came for conversion.
4. A 4-year national conversion schedule called for installing the new system in four branches per region per quarter.
5. Supervised learning by doing would take the place of formal off-the-job training in the new system for branch management.

To effect the behavioral change in the first-line supervisor the consultant had a two-pronged plan. The "information and exhortation" phase of the plan called for an orientation period of two or three days just prior to conversion for the branch management in each branch. This orientation was based on very detailed "Guides" written for each position, explaining what the changes were to be and why they were designed.

The second phase of the consultant's conversion plan involved "engineering" the field of forces that molded the first-line supervisor's behavior. These planned alterations are sketched below:

Environmental Context—Little was done, or could be in the short run, with the external economics, the institutional setting, or the internal economics of the company. Nor were there any significant changes in the environmental context during the conversion process that might affect the proposed changes.

Structural Context—Most of the consultant's effort was expended in making systemic alterations as outlined below.

Authority Structure—Two levels were added to the scalar chain of the Personal Life Sales Division, and decentralized management by results replaced centralized procedural control. Within each branch the first-line supervisor was delegated true line authority.

Reward Structure—A new performance measure allowed the installation of a system analogous to the profit center system in each branch. The system also permitted each first-line supervisor to be rewarded and recognized individually, largely on the basis of what his unit of agents produced.

Work-Flow System and Schedule—Without changing the basic branch work flow, the consultant gave the first-line supervisor a more meaningful role. Through scheduled individual conferences with each of his agents, the first-line supervisor involved himself in the planning and controlling of day-to-day agent work flow.

Information-Flow System—A new Branch Marketing Plan based on the new performance measure put the first-line supervisor right at the hub of the information-flow system. He was involved as sender, receiver, processor, and storer of no less than a dozen critically important items in the marketing plan.

Physical Structure—The first-line supervisor was moved from the undifferentiated position in a general workroom to a private office with private phone, and he was provided with a professionally appointed conference room for meetings with his agency unit.

Behavioral Context—The consultant planned alterations in the behavior of branch manager and agents to facilitate the behavioral change of the first-line supervisor. These modifications were to take place simultaneously with the changes in first-line supervisor behavior.

Branch Manager—Critical in the branch manager's new pattern was a change in self-image from a manager of agents to a manager of managers. Such a pattern would necessarily involve the branch manager in much more planning and drastically less contact with agents. Newly proposed dialogue with first-line supervisors would require abandoning formality and dominance in contacts with his subordinates.

Agents—The behavior pattern alteration for the agent hinged on his acceptance of the first-line supervisor as his "boss." He would have to accommodate himself to a new emphasis on personal development in field work with his superior and to a new activity schedule that put him in closer contact with a smaller group of his peers.

The next chapter presents the evidence of the consultant's relative success in changing the first-line supervisor's behavior in the direction of his proposed pattern through the use of the conversion policies and plans presented in this chapter.

CHAPTER SIX

Results of the Conversion Effort

INTRODUCTION

THIS CHAPTER REPORTS the behavior of the regular managers observed after the consultant's plans had been carried out. Reported first is the composite picture of postconversion behavior of the regular managers in offices 1 to 6. Next comes the detailed profile of the individual behavior patterns of the four regular managers in offices 7 and 8. Then the regular manager's postconversion behavior is put into the context of branch manager and regular agent postconversion behavior. (All these data were collected by the researcher.) Finally, measurable performance indices are reported, comparing preconversion to postconversion performance, so that the economic impact of the change can be related to the behavioral impact.

It should be noted right from the start that the findings recorded here reflect results of the conversion effort during what might be called the transition period. The data relating to offices 1 through 6 were collected some 15 months following the official conversion date; the data on offices 7 and 8, some 5 months following conversion. Complete change was not expected immediately, but neither consultant nor client firmly projected the optimal length of the transition. Plans for effecting the change were not altered in any major way before completion of this study, but policy clarifications, revision of some forms and procedures, and refining the information and exhortation program were accomplished by the office of the conversion coordinator under the guidance of the consultant. Just as the field research for this study was being finished, the formal training program for regular managers was being introduced, in part at least, for selected regular managers in a few regions. At that time, too, the company announced changes in the agents' compensation arrangements. Some six months after this study was completed, the consultants—after their own follow-up research—helped in developing guides for regional managers whose regions were fully converted. Obviously, then, the study was not conducted in static laboratory conditions, but the eight offices analyzed experienced substantially the same planned changes. Care is taken in reporting the results—both in terms of the behavior pattern and of the measurable performance indices—to distinguish between the findings in offices 1 through 6 and those in offices 7 and 8. The former material deals in a more general way with 17 regular managers in six offices with about 15 months' experience with the new system. The latter deals more specifically with four regular managers who had about five months' experience in the new system.

REGULAR MANAGER BEHAVIOR PATTERN POSTCONVERSION— OFFICES 1 TO 6 COMPOSITE

In reporting each of the elements of behavior (activities, interactions, and sentiments) , the researcher first indicates the composite pattern from offices 1 to 6, then the individual patterns from offices 7 to 8—a format very much like that used to record preconversion behavior in Chapter Three.

Regular Managers' Activities

All indications pointed to substantially more in-office activity than the 35 percent estimated in the proposed behavior pattern. Caring for records and reports took at least double the time, even after more than a year of practice. Over half the men interviewed had designed a "second set of books" to record performance "for the agent's sake" in terms of commissions earned, as well as in terms of NPM 1. In addition, more than half "kept score" for unit contests and "games," using tote boards or handmade bulletins. Substantial time was spent, too, reconciling and comparing official machine-produced records (recently automated in the home office and subject to the normal debugging errors) with their own records. Individual conferences with agents typically did not take an hour, but they were still scheduled for an hour. The slack time was spent usually in satisfying agent inquiries, exchanging information with clerks, making inquiries to the branch manager, or responding to his inquiries. Activity within the individual conference, for the majority, consisted almost entirely in supervisory inquiry concerning the week's performance—business written and lapse control—with very little time given to planning the next week's activities. Almost half of the regular managers used the planning form provided,[1] and these men consistently did more planning. Most regular managers did spend approximately an hour in unit conference. Very often more than a quarter of the time was dedicated to administrative detail (reporting the week's business by each agent, updating intraunit contest standings, distributing and explaining a new page for the rate book or a new procedure, etc.). Presentation of material prepared in the home office (filmstrips, new sales aids, etc.) often took another half hour or more. More often than not the regular manager used the balance of the conference to tailor the educational message of the home-office materials to his unit's specific needs or to introduce a training or inspirational idea of his own. Activity in the conference wth the branch manager usually coincided with the proposed pattern—check of the past week's performance and plan for the next week's—except that quite often the checking phase consumed well over half the time. Often, therefore, the regular manager spent a disproportionate amount of time responding to specific inquiries about the disposition of specific pieces of business, the chances of revival of particular lapse cases, and so forth. The regular manager used about the estimated amount of time in preparation for the three types of weekly conferences—most of it in preparing for the unit conference and for the individual conference with the branch manager. It has already been pointed out that less than 65 percent of the workweek remained free for the field and clinical training of individual agents. In the utilization of this reduced time there were strong indications that the change from "demonstration selling" to longer range sales training was far from complete. This time was to be used on a priority basis in developing prospecting and selling skills in those men with potential. While this was an often articulated ideal, in practice the regular manager spent a significant fraction

---

[1]The regular manager had the option of using the planning form. See line 7 in Exhibit 5-6.

of this time making conservation calls alone or with an agent. By self-admission and testimony of the agents the balance of the time was heavily weighted with "demonstration selling" by the majority of the regular managers.

The normal workweek described above turned out to be almost an exception for a quarter of the regular managers interviewed. Nonprogrammed activities associated with open agencies caused by disability and termination—particularly the latter—disrupted this normal workweek pattern. First to go was the training-demonstration selling time with the agents. A cut in conference preparation came next. For the six offices from which these data are drawn, Exhibit 6–1 indicates how much nonprogrammed activity incident to open agencies was necessary in the 12 months following conversion.

EXHIBIT 6–1

Terminations and Open Agencies in Offices 1 to 6
During the 12 Months Following Conversion

Office	Number of Terminations*	Number of Open Agencies at Conversion	Number of Weeks with Open Agencies	Number of Weeks with Multiple Open Agencies
1	7	2	45	37
2	4	1	25	2
3	6	1	52	26
4†	6	2	31	10
5	9	0	31	7
6	3	0	18	8

*Takes account of agencies added in offices 2, 3, and 5.
†Data cover 41 weeks after conversion.

Recall the activities associated with open agencies: termination audit for the departing agent; collecting, servicing, and bookkeeping for the open agency; recruiting a replacement (a new responsibility for the regular manager) ; and introducing the new man on the agency (usually a two-week assignment). In four cases there is strong reason to believe the regular manager was a victim of a vicious circle. Open agency activity so occupied his time that he could not adequately service the agents on his unit, so another agent would leave, saddling the regular manager with a double load. In these four cases the regular manager was occupied with nonprogrammed open agency activity for at least one open agency over a continuous period of six months or more. Only a quarter of the men interviewed escaped this chore in the 12 months following conversion. Recruiting in anticipation of open agencies was a rare activity—though the picture was changing quickly—among the sample of 17 regular managers. Only three stood out in this regard.

Recognizing the crucial impact of open agency activity on the normal workweek pattern, we can summarize the results of the efforts to change activities, as shown in Exhibit 6–2.

EXHIBIT 6–2

Observed Postconversion Regular Manager Activities
in Branches 1 to 6 Compared to the Proposed Activity Pattern

Activity	Proposed Time Distribution (percent)	Observed Postconversion Activity Offices 1–6 Composite
Field and clinical training	65	Conservation efforts and demonstration selling outweigh training in a smaller than proposed time allocation
Individual agent	17	About two thirds of this time used—very much more checking than planning
Unit conferences	3	Conforms quite closely to behavior model proposed—especially in educational activity
Individual conferences with branch manager	3	Detailed checking often overbalances planning
Conference preparation	7	Only a small fraction of this time is given to preparation for individual agent conferences
Records and reports	5	Time allocation usually doubled, in part by extra, self-assumed record keeping
Miscellaneous		In-office activity time allocation expanded by unprogrammed information exchanges with branch manager, agents, clerks

Regular Managers' Interactions

In the normal workweek the regular manager spent about two thirds of his time with individual agents, about 70 percent when group interaction is included. When involved in training-demonstration selling activities, the regular manager initiated well over half the contacts. While interaction time in individual agent conferences seemed to be cut by about a third, in-office contact with individual agents on a nonprogrammed basis consumed appreciable time. These short frequent contacts were more often initiated by the agent. In the other individual contacts the regular manager still dominated the initiation, though in a minority of cases the individual conferences came closer to a dialogue. As noted earlier, less than half the regular managers used the planning form which could have been the basis for agent initiation in the conference. In a majority of cases, the regular manager initiated most of the unit conference interaction. Rather consistently, however, dialogue typified a portion, small though it was, of the unit conference. Individual contact with the branch manager seemed to be double the estimate in the proposed behavior pattern. Frequent short interactions, with initiation shared about equally, occurred on a nonprogrammed basis. In the scheduled conference, the branch manager was most frequently the initiator. Interaction programmed in the new information-flow system seemed to occur as planned. However, almost half of the regular managers indicated—with indirect corroboration from the branch manager—that the branch manager took a stronger hand than planned in initiating the critical step in the annual planning process —the determination of unit NPM 1 objectives (see line 3 in Exhibit 5–6). The consultant's plans provided for no programmed peer interaction, but two of the six branches scheduled monthly management meetings. Occasionally, a request for exemption or a complaint from an agent about another agent "pirating my business" would bring regular managers together in other than a social-amenities contact. The regular manager quite often found it necessary to interact with clerks in brief information exchanges more frequently than planned. Interaction time with individual agents suffered most when the regular manager had to be occupied with open agency activities. Results of the conversion effort on interaction patterns in the normal workweek could be summarized as shown in Exhibit 6–3.

Regular Managers' Sentiments

With respect to feeling like a truly responsible manager, regular managers drew an important distinction. All expressed the conviction that they should be fully responsible managers, but a sizable minority chafed under the feeling that the branch manager was not allowing them to act the role completely. In only one branch could the researcher uncover a consistent pattern of "interference" in the regular manager's administration of their units—continual involvement in details of agents' performance, reproving, advising, and pushing. In most of the other cases, the feelings reflected nonrepetitive episodes, concerning which the branch managers in question gen-

EXHIBIT 6-3

Observed Postconversion Regular Manager Interactions in
Branches 1 to 6 Compared to the Proposed Interaction Pattern

Interaction	Proposed Time Distribution (percent)	Observed Postconversion Interactions Offices 1-6 Composite
With individual agents	82	About 15 percent less time allocation and many more frequent and short interactions. Initiation largely dominated by regular manager
With agent group	3	About as planned except for somewhat excessive regular manager initiation
With branch manager alone	3	Time allocation almost doubled by short, frequent contacts, but branch manager often dominates initiation in programmed interaction
With clerks	2	Somewhat increased time allocation in short, frequent contacts

erally expressed somewhat embarrassed sensitivity. In the remaining situations the regular managers seemed to have had unreal expectations behind such comments as "The branch manager is the only one who can contact the home office or regional manager" and "All the mail—even the material for me—from the home office or regional office is addressed to the branch manager." All considered, the regular managers behaved toward their agents as if they viewed themselves as responsible line managers.

With the design of the compensation arrangement the consultant tried to induce a balanced concern for the production of new business and the conservation of existing business. Both certainly concerned the regular manager, though he expressed uneasiness about the proper balance of emphasis. He was hypersensitive to the point that a dollar of business lost (no matter how long in force) meant as much to him as a dollar of new business—the former could negate the latter. Yet the agent, because of his compensation contract, weighted a dollar of new business more than ten times the importance of a dollar of business that had been on the books a year or more. This gap between the reward structures produced a tension with which most regular managers had a hard time living.[2]

---

[2]The change in agent compensation, announced as this research ended, contained a feature designed to alleviate this situation, concerning which both consultant and client long had been aware.

The consultant wished to instill a long-term view of manpower development in the place of an overriding concern for the immediate sale. Regular managers were to put a premium on men who had potential. Only a minority acted out the conviction expressed by the majority. The roadblock was agent expectation. All expected "more personal attention" from the regular manager. Compounding the difficulty was the traditionally protected position of the veteran agent. The continuation of "demonstration selling" reflects the pressure of agent expectation. In the hiring of new men, however, regular managers often showed the strength of this conviction in multiplying selection interviews in the search for the right man, rather than just "plugging the hole with any warm body."

A fourth sentiment in the proposed behavior was that the regular manager retain a measure of branch spirit and management team loyalty as he built up his own unit. Since units were independent in normal day-to-day operations, the real test of management team spirit came in periods of abnormal operations—particularly when a brother regular manager labored under open agency pressure. With a single open agency a regular manager almost invariably handled all the nonprogrammed activities and the necessarily curtailed programmed activities by himself. Such was generally the case, too, when a regular manager had two open agencies. In two cases where regular managers had three open agencies simultaneously, no help was forthcoming from the management team.[3] In one case of a multiple open agency situation the branch manager assigned help to the burdened regular manager. There was much more protestation of willingness to help a brother regular manager (admittedly out of enlightened self-interest—"I might need help next"—rather than altruism) than there was concrete evidence of such help. In the one case where the researcher observed such voluntary assistance, the regular manager who was beneficiary was perturbed:

Last year when 3D had three open agencies I offered to help him. Last year 3B had an open agency too and I helped him. So this year when I have three open agencies they volunteered to help me. After all, we all share in the branch pot. However, everything is not as rosy as this volunteer spirit

---

[3]In the *Regular Manager's Guide* a multiple open agencies situation constitutes an emergency: "Regular Managers will be assigned to assume branch responsibilities in addition to those of their units when emergency situations demand. . . . Such emergency assistance will be limited to an absolute minimum but should be expected from all Regular Managers. Branch Managers will rotate such emergency assistance among Regular Managers at weekly intervals to avoid imposing on any one manager or unit."

seems to make it. Under the old system there was a true spirit of cooperation when a man worked with you. Now take this book on my desk, for instance. A brother regular manager volunteered to work that book (collect the agency) for me, but just before you came in he dropped the book on my desk with all the payments yet to be entered. He just dropped the book and told me I could do the bookkeeping. He did the collecting but did not complete the job. The spirit of cooperation has changed, there's no doubt about it!

Other evidences of cooperation were lacking too. The researcher found no case where one regular manager, voluntarily or by request, made an educational contribution in a unit conference of another regular manager. The researcher found no evidence of joint efforts to develop a pool of prospective agents for any regular manager who might have an open agency. The topic generally prompted a cynical "You're kidding!" It was rather a revealing commentary that only one of the regular managers interviewed came closer than five percentage points in guessing the share of his total income derived from the branch pool.

Finally, the consultant hoped the regular manager would find his new position to have attractive career prospects. Undoubtedly, some regular managers would still anxiously aspire to climb the promotion ladder further, but the short-sighted way-station attitude and the attitude that used to inspire assistant managers to return to agent status would hopefully disappear. Generally, this was the case. Turn-over statistics demonstrated the last point. The regular manager was too conscious of the New Performance Measure to engage in the short-term "wheeling and dealing" of "paper-hanging" that might have been possible under the system in which he was largely evaluated on the basis of the "writings" record appearing on the weekly Form 09. He could not escape from the responsibility for the seven or eight men who were permanently assigned to his unit. Two clouds did hang over the career prospects of the regular manager position. First, after the honeymoon effect of the promotion to regular manager, many were taking a second look at their relative position in the branch hierarchy. The special manager—formerly a peer in every sense—enjoyed symbols of differentiation that seemed to subordinate the regular manager. The differentiating symbols that reshaped the status, if not the authority, structure were direct access to clerical aides in administering his unit, a 25 percent base pay differential, and seemingly higher total earnings potential without the exposure to the bothersome open agency activities (the special agents did no collecting). Many regular managers perceived that this change in status colored the career attractiveness of their positions. Those with promotion ambitions, too, enviously saw the special managers as having the inside track to the branch manager's chair. In two offices the tension between special and regular managers was so evident that embarrassed efforts were made to explain it away. The second cloud over the career attractiveness of the regular manager position was the policy on manpower growth in the branch. A perceptive minority anticipated difficulty if the branch manager planned growth by adding another unit by taking untapped market areas from existing units. In so doing the branch manager might make it impossible for a regular manager to enlarge his own unit under the policy that he could have as many agents on his unit as he could handle. It was seen as a threat to the career attractiveness of the regular manager position if he did not have some rights in the planning of manpower growth.

REGULAR MANAGER (7A, 7B, 8A, 8B) BEHAVIOR PATTERN POSTCONVERSION

The regular managers used in forming the above composite picture had about 15 months' experience with the new system. The four regular managers studied in offices 7 and 8 had five months of experience.

Individual Regular Manager Activities

Activities—7A. This regular manager worked regularly about a 15 percent longer normal workweek than the researcher observed as the average. The distribution of his time came closest to the proposed pattern of all those observed. His individual conferences with the 10 agents on his unit averaged about 40 minutes, some only 20 minutes, a few well over an hour. He utilized the planning form with each agent, reviewing specific performance against plan and plotting the next week's work on the experience of last week's. Rather subtly, 7A wove into the checking and planning activities little training lessons. Each case discussed was the jump-off point for a prospecting or selling tip. What made this individualized detail possible was the half hour or more 7A spent in preparation for each conference. In slack time between conferences or late afternoon "dead" periods, especially Friday PM, he would study each agent's performance record, the mix of business he sold, the type of prospect he had success with, and so forth. Often he would take the agent's account book in the search for success patterns or opportunities. Rarely did an agent leave a conference with his planning form exactly as it was before the conference. The same type of meticulous preparation went into the agenda for the unit conference. The two hours observed by the researcher was common practice attested to by superior, peers, and subordinates alike. The unit conference itself ran a little over an hour and was heavily education oriented. In about 40 minutes 7A led the discussion of methods for closing sales, the use of a new chart (sales aid), multiple sales, and preferred leads. Interspersed in the discussion were numerous personal experiences or queries from agents. The balance of the conference was used to recognize top performers of the week, encourage better lapse control, and reward (with a new shirt or "bottle") agents who had 100 percent of their writings objective for the previous month. 7A set aside about two hours of early Friday afternoon for reports and record keeping.

Since the branch manager did not hold individual conferences with his regular managers, 7A completed all necessary business with him in short "stand-up" sessions that occurred about twice a day. Some business also was conducted at luncheon sessions that occurred once or twice a week. The 60 percent of the workweek remaining was spent in "demonstration selling" with the oldest agent on the unit. This regular manager pointed out—with corroboration from the agents—that he typically sold for the older men on the unit but spent the field time with the younger men in rather formal training.

Activities—7B. Individual agent conferences consumed about 25 percent of 7B's normal workweek. Typically, he would spend an hour or more with most of his 10 agents. With half of them—the younger men—he used the planning form. During the conference the planning and checking elements were present, but prolonged informal conversation was sparked by reference to particular policyholders, prospects, policies, and the like. The researcher could not judge whether this extensive conversation was productive. This regular manager did not seem to, or profess to, specifically prepare for the conferences, though he did spend more total time in record keeping than estimated in the proposed behavior pattern. Record keeping and tote-board posting for a special unit sales contest accounted for part of this increased time. He did spend about an hour preparing his unit conference. In the hour-long unit conference over half the time was occupied with inspirational readings from a book, *Conviction* (which 7B had all his agents purchase), and with the trading of stories about insurance as an institution. For five minutes the unit tossed around ideas about the local market potential for annuities. The regular manager took the balance of time to announce the weekly writing leaders and to appeal for more effort to conserve business. As with 7A, this regular manager conducted his business with the branch manager in nonprogrammed contacts. In this case, however, they were longer and more frequent. Information exchanges with clerks consumed something over an hour during the week. It was not uncommon for 7B to engage in business oriented small talk with agents in the office or coffee shop for as much as an hour a day. During the week of observation 7B spent an hour and a half with a prospective agent for a new agency soon to be created. Less than 50 percent of the workweek remained for field work with the agents. During the particular week when the researcher was present, conservation calls accounted for over half this field time. More generally, 7B used this time for "demonstration selling."

Note that neither 7A nor 7B had any nonprogrammed, open agency activity since conversion.

Activities—8A. The open agency 8A inherited at the time of conversion remained open at the time of the researcher's follow-up visit. Hence, 8A did not have a normal week of activity. Almost 40 percent of the workweek went to collect and service the open agency in a distant suburb. He could manage only 15 percent of his time (on two late afternoons and early evenings) for "demonstration selling" with one of his agents. Individual conferences with his seven agents averaged a half hour and were largely occupied with checking in detail the previous week's performance by a review of the planning form he required of all the agents. Planning was restricted to a cursory look to verify that the agent in fact had prepared his plan. Though the unit meeting the researcher observed lasted 45 minutes, those involved agreed an hour was more typical. Administrative detail (handing out and discussing three new pages for the rate book and distributing career extension course diplomas) took 25 minutes. Unplanned discussion of competitive annuities and term insurance plans occupied the balance of the conference. The weekly conference with the branch manager took a little more than an hour. After a

15-minute review of the past week's performance, 8A and the branch manager discussed new agent selection policy—what minimum test scores to require on the basis of the branch's turnover experience. The researcher could not identify any specific conference preparation other than the two hours typically spent in record keeping and report making. Neither could the researcher identify how 8A typically spent the remaining 30 percent of the workweek. In the week observed, 8A used this time, including the slack time between agent conferences, helping two agents who were having trouble balancing their monthly accounts. All that could be learned was that this time was typically in-office time.

Activities—8B. This regular manager, too, was involved with an open agency during the week of observation, as he had been for the previous three months. This particularly difficult agency in a poor metropolitan section required 50 percent or more of 8B's time. Still, 8B managed to spend 25 percent of his time with his newest agent in a combination of sales training in the field and "demonstration selling." Individual agent conferences with his eight men averaged about a half hour. He utilized conference time just about as his brother regular manager did, emphasizing supervisory checks with rather perfunctory planning. The unit conference ran just over a half hour—somewhat shorter than normal. Two thirds of it was spent in handing out and discussing two home office circulars on accident and health insurance. A three-minute visit by the branch manager to present an agent with a diploma from an industry correspondence course prompted a short discussion of continuing educational opportunities. Regular Manager 8B had a shorter than usual conference with the Branch Manager—just a half hour. The discussion revolved about the same selection topic that occupied 8A and the branch manager. Though the researcher only observed a half-hour's conference (unit conference) preparation, 8B insisted that weekly chore normally took an hour or more. He did keep careful records, however—an exercise that consumed almost double the estimate in the proposed pattern. Frequent information exchanges with clerks totaled to about an hour during the week (see Exhibit 6–4).

Individual Regular Manager Interactions

Interactions—7A. This regular manager spent three quarters of his workweek with individual agents, 15 percent across the desk. In

EXHIBIT 6–4

Percent of Workweek Actually Spent in Various
Activities Compared to Proposed Pattern

Activity	Proposed Percent Time Allocated	Postconverson Percent Time Allocation by:			
		7A	7B	8A	8B
Field and clinical training	65				
Demonstration selling		60	20	15	25
Conservation			25		
Individual agent conferences	17	15	25	10	10
Unit conferences	3	3	3	3	2
Conference with branch manager	3			3	2
Conference preparation	7	15	2		
Records and reports	5	5	8	5	9
Open agency activity				40	50
Miscellaneous		2	17	24	2

the field he could be said to have initiated most of the interaction
because he was in command during the "demonstration selling"
activity with the older agent. As pointed out, this activity pattern
changes with the younger men, so the initiations would then also
shift closer to a 50-50 basis. This regular manager's schedule was
arranged so that field time could be planned for large blocks at a
time. The individual conference time with the agents was as close
to a dialogue as witnessed anywhere, as was the hour spent in unit
conference. The brief and frequent contacts with the branch manager summed to about an hour in the week and tended to be initiated
by the branch manager. 7A had no more than passing contact with
his peers and only a couple of contacts with the clerks other than
normal paper flow.

Interactions—7B. Between field and office contacts, 7B spent over
80 percent of his workweek with individual agents. In-office interaction, during conferences or not, 7B typically participated in conversations where initiations seemed to be balanced. This changed
somewhat in the field where 7B assumed a more dominant role in
the conservation and "demonstration selling" activities. In the unit
conference, too, 7B initiated more often than not. One singular
aspect of 7B's contact with agents was the number of different agents
involved during the week, especially in the unprogrammed interactions. He would converse at length with regular agents as well as
with special agents who were not on his unit. About 5 percent of
his time was spent in contact with the branch manager twice a day

or more. Initiation was about equally shared, as it was in the frequent contacts with clerks.

Interactions—8A. Because of the open agency duties, 8A could only spend 50 percent of his time with individual agents—a large fraction of this being nonprogrammed contact with a particular agent who was having account trouble. It seemed less time was allocated to individual agent contact normally. In all of this individual contact—in the field, in conference, or in a special situation—8A dominated the initiation. He tended to do the same in the unit conference, though agents did make contributions. On the other hand, 8A initiated much less frequently than the branch manager did in their weekly conference. 8A had only a few fleeting contacts with clerks aside from the time spent making the twice-a-week deposit of the open agency collections.

Interactions—8B. This regular manager, too, could give substantially less time than proposed to individual agents because of the open agency burden. In the 35 percent of his time he did give them, he almost dominated initiations during field time and initiated well over half the time during conferences. Such was true also in unit conferences, but the reverse was true in the weekly conference with the branch manager. Open agency deposits required 8B to spend an hour or more with clerks (see Exhibit 6–5).

EXHIBIT 6–5

Percent of Workweek Actually Spent Interacting
with Various People Compared to Proposed Pattern

With	Proposed Percent Time Allocated	Postconversion Percent Time Allocation by:			
		7A	*7B*	*8A*	*8B*
Individual agents	82	74	82	49	35
Agent group	3	3	3	3	2
Branch manager alone	3	3	5	2	2
Clerks	2	1	2	2	2

Sentiments of the Individual Regular Managers

It will be easiest to arrange this section topically, relating the attitudes of the four regular managers under each of the five key sentiments outlined in the proposed behavior pattern.

The message about being true line managers with responsibility for end results of a unit of agents came through loud and clear. For example, in the researcher's presence 7A informed his weakest agent that he would have to maintain a certain "writings" minimum for each of the next 10 weeks and achieve a specified minimum target of NPM 1 in the next two-month period or he was through. His brother regular manager, 7B, planned the addition of a new agency on his unit and won the support of the branch manager to his self-initiated proposal. In branch 8 the regular managers had been on their own for some time prior to conversion anyway. Both 8A and 8B were doing their own recruiting and exercising initiative in insisting on rigid selection standards. There was no "passing the buck" to the branch manager, even under the difficult open agency situation. Because of instances in the past where the regular managers felt they had to fight battles alone with the home office (one of which the researcher observed in the preconversion study), 8A and 8B did aspire for more top-level support. This became a serious concern at the time of conversion when these regular managers felt that advice from the regional office was responsible for setting NPM 1 objectives too high (the objectives were adjusted after two months).

Undoubtedly, these regular managers behaved as if they were aware of the importance of both new business and conservation. The question of a balanced interest is clouded by the agents' reaction to any special concern for anything other than first-year lapse. As pointed out earlier, the agent and management compensation arrangements (later changed for the agent) seemed to produce a motivational gap. 7A talked a good deal about lapse control in both agent and unit conferences, but his orientation in field assignments with the agents was the production of new business. He would only "chase lapses" personally in extraordinary cases. 7B, on the other hand, spent half of his field time during the week of observation "chasing lapses." Though this time allocation was found to be somewhat atypical, it was indicative of 7B's attitude. During his unit conference he pleaded for tighter lapse control "because these second-year lapses are killing my income, boys!" In branch 8, the agents rather cynically asked: "Which do you think the regular manager would do, help one agent land a $120 piece of new business or chase a $150 second-year lapse?" As far as the researcher could see, this cynicism was based not so much on distribution of regular manager field time spent on conservation as it was on the emphasis given conservation in individual agent conferences. As pointed out earlier, both 8A and 8B tended to do more checking than planning in these individual sessions.

There is mixed evidence in the area of adopting a longer term view in manpower and market development—developing resources with the most potential for positioning in the most promising markets. 7A spoke with conviction about spending his time with those agents who showed evidence of helping themselves. In a negative way he was consistent with this sentiment when he refused to help the agent whom he placed on 10-week probation. However, the development of potential could not have motivated him to spend the whole week of observation with an agent who was within two years of retirement. 7B showed dramatic evidence of a long-term view when he planned the addition of a new agency in a prime market. Yet, 7B's distribution of field time showed no special attention to development of agents with the most potential. It is appropriate to mention here that during the preconversion orientation sessions, when the regular managers designed the new units (in branch 7, two "equal" units to be assigned to 7A and 7B by lot), potential of both agent and agency was a major criterion. It took 7A and 7B six hours to arrange 20 agents so as to comprise two "equal" units, each of which would be accepted in a chance draw. The only evidence concerning the strength of this longer-term view in the cases of 8A and 8B was their insistence that the recruits for their open agencies be men who scored well on the selection tests and seemed to have stability. There was no consistent evidence that either regular manager determined priorities for time utilization chiefly on the basis of the development needs of men with the most potential. In the design of units, 8A and 8B (with their cohort 8C) tended to lose sight of agent and agency potential in a welter of other criteria—past performance, geography, personalities, and the like.

The balance of branch and unit spirit was really untested in branch 7. It had experienced no open agencies or other emergencies that would have called for regular manager cooperation. Unit pride led 7A to feel slighted (and express this hurt to the branch manager) when 7B got permission for the new agency, thereby upsetting the balance of two 10-man units. Rather sharp banter on weekly unit performance indicated a new form of competition within the branch. Nonetheless, 7A willingly agreed to handle any major problems on 7B's unit during 7B's vacation (7B had delegated all of his normal duties to one of his senior agents). In a somewhat dramatic agreement sealed with a handshake the night they designed the units, the regular managers in branch 8 promised voluntarily to help one another if and when the need should arise. Two of the three (the one not specifically studied in this research had a full unit) had open agencies almost from the start. One day when 8B was sick, 8C offered to collect on the open agency. In recruiting, 8A and 8B did check with one another about each prospect. Other than these instances, there was no evidence of cooperation or proffered help. On the other hand, 8B was quite disturbed when one of his agents requested, with support from 8C, to switch units and fill an expected open agency on 8C's unit. By procedure, the move would be made only when 8C produced an agent prospect acceptable to 8B in filling the opening created on his unit. 8B felt pressured to agree but thought 8C was pulling a "shrewd deal" by getting a seasoned agent who would require no special introductory training, while 8B would have an introduction added to his already burdensome open agency duties. 8B felt further hurt when the special manager offered to sell him for $10 each the names of any prospects he might find in his own search for special agents who looked more like regular agent material than special agent material. There seemed to be no competitive tensions between branch 8 units in terms of weekly sales.

Finally, these regular managers had generally suspended judgment on the career attractiveness of their new jobs until they had more concrete evidence of the earning potential. 7A was the only one who had strong drives for promotion. He would never be satisfied at the regular manager level. It chafed him to think that the special manager would probably have first try at promotion. His brother regular manager, 7B, found appreciable comfort in being promoted from assistant manager to regular manager. He, more than the others, considered this a career position. Still, in the researcher's presence, 7B asked the regional manager if there was not some chance that a true assistant branch manager position might not be created. 7B had subbed for the branch manager on many occasions in the past but saw the creation of the special manager position as a threat to his "number two" status. In branch 8, 8A looked upon the new position of regular manager as further security for the few remaining years he had before retirement. On the other hand, 8B feared "dog-eat-dog" competition among regular managers so much that he was quietly taking an educational psychology course one night a week so that he might prepare himself for a teaching position as a hedge.

POSTCONVERSION BEHAVIORAL CONTEXT

Having seen, toward the end of Chapter 4, the behavior of the branch manager and regular agent as part of the basic influences on assistant manager behavior before conversion and, in Chapter 5, the consultant's plans to alter the behavioral context as a determinant of regular manager behavior, it is fitting here to relate briefly the character of the behavioral context after conversion. Below is a composite picture of branch manager and regular agent behavior drawn from branches 1 to 6 with specific additions from branches 7 and 8.

The Branch Manager

Branch Manager activity became very unstructured after conversion, so much so that branch managers have difficulty explaining how they spend their time. Conferences with each of their regular and special managers seemed to be the cohesive force for the workweek. These conferences consumed more total time than the managers' meeting and the general meeting that were part of the old system. In the conferences, "checking the record" seemed to take more than half of the hour, but planning for the next week's activities did receive attention by all. Only branch manager 7 did not schedule conferences with his regular and special managers. In addition to the data processing, recording, and reporting incident to the new branch marketing plan, most branch managers maintained—at least in modified form—the record-keeping procedures they were accustomed to under the old system. These information-handling activities, largely geared toward preparation for the conferences with the regular and special managers, often consumed more than one quarter of the branch manager's time. There was evidence in all but two of the eight branches that the branch manager occasionally attended unit conferences. The researcher only observed this on two occasions. In branch 8 the branch manager was present in the 8B's unit conference just long enough to hand out a diploma. In branch 7 the branch manager virtually took over a conference of special agents for the presentation of an especially complex technical point. With this slight evidence the researcher could not judge the character of the activity the branch manager engaged in while attending these unit conferences. Unplanned information exchanges with regular and special managers and with clerks consumed a little more time in the new system than in the old one—partly because clerical procedures were being revised as the result of the second consulting assignment. Some branch managers had shifted some of the policyholder inquiries to regular managers, but generally such activity still required the same time from the branch manager. Long-range planning for new offices in three cases, and for growth generally, seemed to take an increasing portion of the branch manager's time. In summary, the branch manager lived in a less structured world and was outside of most of the branch work flow. The fact that one branch manager said, "My golf score is improving," and another said, "The most important thing I do around here is keep the pamphlet rack full," is commentary on the researcher's general observation—the branch manager under the new system was not pressed for time.

The branch manager's interaction pattern changed most dramatically in the number of contacts with agents, the total time spent with agents, and the direction of typical initiation in interactions with agents. In almost every case the number of contacts and total time were reduced by over a half, and the initiation shifted almost entirely to the agent's hands. Individual contact with the regular managers now replaced the group contact of the Thursday managers' meeting. This individual interaction with regular and special managers, inside and outside of weekly conferences, consumed a quarter or more of the branch manager's week. In these contacts the branch manager seemed to dominate the initiation, though in all but one branch there seemed to be at least some dialogue. Other than the paper-flow interaction programmed in the Branch Marketing Plan, the branch manager had limited contact with the regional manager once conversion was accomplished. Most branch managers classified their contacts with their immediate supervisor as fire-fighting sessions, mostly by phone. They felt he was too busy with his conversion schedule to have time for branches already converted. In any event, the branch manager himself handled virtually all the contact with the regional or home office (outside of the normal paper flow in the writing-placing cycle) .

In sentiment, all but one of the branch managers had modified the

"I run the whole show" attitude. They let the regular managers make decisions (on hiring, on the allocation of time with agents, on agenda for unit meetings, etc.) that customarily were within only the branch manager's competence under the old system. The branch manager's involvement with detail about specific cases of new or lapse business bothered some regular managers. Concentration on such specifics in conferences led these regular managers to complain of too-close supervision. In an embarrassed fashion, five of the eight branch managers cited examples of where they had not "stepped back" and given their regular managers free rein. This sensitivity reflects a substantial shift in sentiment. Unfortunately, the researcher could not observe branch managers in action during the annual objective-setting period, which would be the real test of the branch manager's willingness to delegate. There is evidence that some branch managers may have gone too far in putting the regular managers on their own. Branch Manager 8 would be the prime example here, but his health probably dictated the "virtual abdication." In other cases, however, branch managers were so conscious of "stepping back" that they did not give regular managers support, even in emergency situations. It was the branch manager's responsibility to determine when an emergency situation existed (usually when multiple open or disability agencies burdened one regular manager). More often than not, the branch manager "stepped back" and let the regular manager "work through his own problems and learn by the experience." It did seem in four or five of these cases that the branch manager was more concerned with "stepping back" than he was sensitive to the deleterious effects of open agency situations on the unit as a whole. Finally, the upgrading of the regular manager position did not level the perceived status of the branch manager. The regular manager's physical appointments and salary expectations still allowed the branch manager a big edge in differentiating symbols. There was some relaxation of the regular manager's practice of calling the branch manager "Mister _____."

The Regular Agent

The new staggered deposit and unit conference schedule changed the in-office activity pattern of the agent somewhat. The time he would have to have spend queuing for check-off and deposit twice a week under the old system was now partly spent in the weekly in-. dividual conference with the regular manager. Some of the better (measured in production terms) agents found more time for field activities under the new system, but generally agents seemed to spend about the same time in the office.

Agent interaction patterns have changed especially in relation to the branch manager, as indicated above. In the unit conferences, more agents participated more frequently than in the old general meeting. The interaction time formerly spent with the branch manager and with the several assistant managers now shifted to interaction with one regular manager consistently—this in the scheduled individual conferences, where there was at least some dialogue, and in the frequent nonprogrammed in-office contacts the agent generally initiated. Total field interaction time with the regular managers was fairly significantly reduced in most cases, though more agents had shorter field contacts with the regular manager in any one month than under the old system. The initiation pattern in the field contacts had not appreciably changed.

One last significant change in the agent interaction pattern was the loosening of social peer groupings as a result of the new schedule that programmed office activity for different units at different times, instead of the former arrangement where all agents were in the office together twice a week. When the group was present, an agent could and did interact more frequently with any of his peers without regard to staff assignment. In the new system, the agent had to "choose his friends" from a smaller group, the unit, which was formed completely without his influence. Once assigned to a unit he could not switch. The physical arrangement of assigned personal desks that was at times conducive to peer group formation was now gone, too. Some few cliques divided by the new unit arrangement and separated by the new staggered schedule created opportunities to be together in the office, in the coffee shop, or in off-the-job social settings. More generally, however, some new allegiances were formed within the unit, or agents tended to lose identification with peer groups and became "loners." This flux was evident even in the researcher's brief visits to offices 1 to 6 some 15 months after conversion. In offices 7 and 8 the splintering of peer groups was quite evident. Note in Exhibits 6–6 and 6–7 how the new unit divisions separated peer group members, making frequent interaction of "friends" more difficult. (These are the same peer groups

EXHIBIT 6–6

Diagram Showing the Impact of the New Unit Assignments
of Agents on the Peer Groups in Branch 7

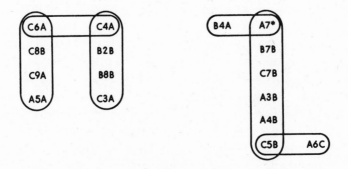

EXHIBIT 6–7

Diagram Showing the Impact of the New Unit Assignments
of Agents on the Peer Groups in Branch 8

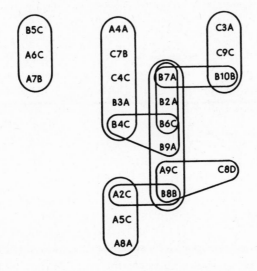

identified before conversion—see Exhibits 4–9 and 4–10. The first
letter and number identify the staff assignments prior to conversion.
The second letter indicates the unit assignment after conversion.)

This social upheaval explains in part the somewhat strong sentiments of many of the agents. The unit spirit, so much hoped for, was
slow in coming. Agents missed what they themselves called the
"country-club atmosphere" associated with the twice-a-week general
gathering in the office. Intraunit contests did generate some unit

spirit. Regular managers felt interunit competition much more than the agents. In a more subtle way, agents missed the recognition of applause from 30 of their peers (instead of 7 or 8) and sensed a motivational vacuum in the smaller unit conferences. The branch manager was generally a professional in generating "electricity" in the larger group, sparking motivation and inspiration. The regular manager who could match this in the smaller group was rare indeed. He had to substitute a lower key form of recognition, motivation, and inspiration (which would be more effective in the long run anyway, insisted client and consultant). While a few of the older agents saw the regular manager as a "young pup," and some of the more productive agents resisted ceding status to a regular manager who never outproduced them, most agents accepted the regular manager as their "boss." Many more agents aspired to the regular manager rank, including some who had stepped down from the former assistant manager position. Finally, and most important, the agent expectation of what the regular manager would do for him seemed somewhat out of phase with reality. The agents were "sold" the new system on the basis that they would get "more personal attention from the regular manager." The agent translated that promise to mean "I will get more field assignment time and hence more help in direct selling from the regular manager." In point of fact, the regular manager would have less time for field work than the assistant manager, and he was instructed to use field time more for training than "demonstration selling." Because of this misconstrued anticipation, the agents put considerable pressure on regular managers for more "demonstration selling" time.

PERFORMANCE INDICES

The consultant proposed changes in behavior pattern to achieve measurable improvements in performance. It was expected that there would be a time lag in such improvement, but this section records some interim results.

Interim Results in Branches 1 to 6

Using the New Performance Measure, a comparison can be drawn between the performance in the three quarters immediately preceding conversion (the first three quarters of 1962) and quarters 2,

3, and 4 following conversion (the first three quarters of 1963). While the picture is mixed, there is significant improvement (see Exhibit 6–8) in three of the five branches.

EXHIBIT 6–8

Changes in NPM 1 and Expenses per Dollar of NPM 1
Before and after Conversion*

Branch†	Percent Increase in NPM 1 in Postconversion Period	Expenses per Dollar of NPM 1 under or Over Standard	
		1962	1963
1	34	0.15 over	0.06 under
2	36	0.30 over	0.03 over
3	9	0.03 over	0.03 under
5	(16) ‡	0.05 under	0.09 over
6	(27)	0.01 under	0.14 over

*The larger sample, including these five offices, showed a 19 percent increase in NPM 1 in the postconversion period and showed an improvement in expenses per dollar of NPM 1 from 0.07 over standard before conversion to 0.07 below standard after conversion.
†Branch 4 data not available.
‡( )Denotes decrease.

Exhibit 6–9 gives a closer look at the trend in lapse control a year before and a year after conversion, year-to-date figures presented at half-year intervals. Conversion date was October 1962. The numbers are factored, but the lower the number, the better the lapse control. In branches 5 and 6 the picture has worsened. In the other branches two points should be noted. There is generally more improvement in the conservation of notice business (the type the company would like to emphasize more) and generally better improvement in total net lapse control (which includes business on the books more than a year), probably reflecting the change in management compensation that penalizes managers equally for all lapses.

A study of how the agencies of individual regular manager's units produced the year after conversion compared to production of NPM 1 the year prior to conversion provides some insights. Recall that a regular manager had a different group of agencies on his unit after conversion than he did on his staff before conversion. Exhibit 6–10 shows the aggregate production of each regular manager's unit as if the same agencies were grouped together before conversion. It also shows how the regular manager's compensation changed in the same period. The sample includes regular managers who were interviewed

EXHIBIT 6–9
Lapse Rates before and after Conversion
(Conversion Date: October 1962)

	Account Business		Notice Business	
	First-Year Net Lapse	Total Net Lapse	First-Year Net Lapse	Total Net Lapse
Branch 1				
October 1961	0.090	3.077	0.049	2.528
March 1962	0.123	3.007	0.092	2.103
September 1962	0.106	2.897	0.089	2.329
March 1963	0.122	2.424	0.053	1.639
September 1963	0.097	2.255	0.071	2.144
Branch 2				
October 1961	0.119	2.483	0.086	2.276
March 1962	0.160	3.167	0.098	2.319
September 1962	0.119	2.502	0.082	2.255
March 1963	0.119	1.527	0.102	1.859
September 1963	0.099	1.989	0.087	1.823
Branch 3				
October 1961	0.098	2.479	0.067	2.449
March 1962	0.129	2.529	0.073	2.097
September 1962	0.158	2.929	0.080	2.133
March 1963	0.149	2.871	0.056	1.658
September 1963	0.145	2.666	0.063	1.823
Branch 5				
October 1961	0.104	2.558	0.058	1.773
March 1962	0.099	2.157	0.059	1.453
September 1962	0.083	2.186	0.068	1.839
March 1963	0.135	2.307	0.094	1.791
September 1963	0.103	2.106	0.094	1.864
Branch 6				
October 1961	0.067	2.566	0.033	1.970
March 1962	0.132	2.834	0.062	2.381
September 1962	0.104	3.018	0.060	2.270
March 1963	0.116	2.087	0.066	2.290
September 1963	0.099	2.685	0.091	2.555

by the researcher and for whose agencies sufficient comparable data were available. (See Appendix IV for detail by agency.)

Immediately obvious in Exhibit 6–10 is the fact that the regular manager position brought virtually an automatic raise in pay.[4] Obvious, too, is the slump in business generated by the agencies in the 12 months following conversion—though it should be pointed out that this sample is somewhat worse than the average. Also note that a later study by the consultant shows that an upswing substantially better than company average occurs in the second year and thereafter.

---

[4] Company research on a larger sample shows that, while this may be true in some cases, it is not true on the average.

EXHIBIT 6–10

Comparison of Unit Performance and Regular Manager
Compensation—Year before versus Year after Conversion

	Percent Change in NPM 1 By Unit—Year before versus Year after Conversion	Percent Change in Regular Manager's Compensation Year before versus Year After Conversion
1A	(20.0) *	12.8
1C	14.0†	15.8
2A	(23.0)	18.3
2C	(44.0) §	71.5‖
3B	(16.5)	24.1
3C	80.0	42.6
3D	(106.0)	10.1
5B	(29.0)	14.2
5C	(5.5)	7.5
5D	(34.0) #	6.9
6B	(27.0)	11.4

( )Denotes decrease.
*Data unavailable for two of the nine agencies.
†New agency, added after conversion, produced double the company average NPM 1.
§Data unavailable for two of the eight agencies.
‖Served as agent for one quarter of the year before conversion.
#New agency, added after conversion, produced about the average company NPM 1.

Part of the reason for the slump undoubtedly is traceable to open
agencies. The researcher visited the branches in question three to
four months after the end of the year following conversion. At that
time, brief observation of these regular managers and interviews
with them and their superiors, peers, and subordinates led the researcher to infer the following from the data in Exhibit 6–10. First,
there generally is, indeed, a lag between converted regular manager
behavior (relative conformity with the proposed behavior pattern)
and measurable performance improvement. The two regular managers of this group who seemed to conform most closely to the proposed behavior pattern—3B and 5D—did not enjoy the best results.
Even at the time of the researcher's visit, they were not leaders,
though both were just about 100 percent of their unit objectives. The
three regular managers whose behavior seemed to deviate most from
the proposed pattern—3C, 5B, and 6B—did not show the worst results.
As a matter of fact, 3C showed the best results in the year following
conversion—allegedly because he was able to produce very well himself in "demonstration selling" assignments. By dint of similar, obviously exhaustive, effort, 3C was 92 percent of his objective in the
first quarter of 1964 despite the fact that he had three open agencies

During the week of the researcher's visit, 5B resigned, with his unit just 25 percent of objective. 6B was doing somewhat better at 75 percent of objective, but he was seriously considering early retirement. The second inference would then be that a regular manager whose behavior deviates significantly from the proposed pattern seems to face a cumulating pressure. These pressures tell on the man and eventually on his unit performance.

Interim Results in Branches 7 and 8

In the last three quarters of 1964, the period following conversion, branches 7 and 8 showed increases in the personal-life sector of NPM 1 over the comparable period in the year before conversion. Both showed an improvement in the expenses per dollar of growth index as shown in Exhibit 6–11.

EXHIBIT 6–11
Changes in NPM 1 and Expenses per Dollar
of NPM 1 before and after Conversion

		Expense per Dollar of NPM 1 under and Over Standard	
Branch	*Percent Increase in NPM 1 In Postconversion Period*	*Before*	*After*
7	8.0	0.06 under	0.12 under
8	3.2	0.30 over	0.03 under

These two branches showed improvement, too, in lapse control after conversion, as did the other branches cited in Exhibit 6–9. Branch 7 did somewhat better than branch 8 and was more consistent with the trends noted in Exhibit 6–9. That is, branch 7 showed good improvement in total net lapse in notice business as well as in account business (see Exhibit 6–12).

Exhibit 6–13 gives some idea of the relative success achieved by the four regular managers closely observed in branches 7 and 8. Here, just as in Exhibit 6–10 for branches 1 to 6, it is assumed for comparison's sake that each regular manager was assigned the same agencies before conversion as after conversion. Only under the aegis of regular manager 7A (whose behavior conformed most closely with the proposed pattern) did the agencies show improvement in the three quarters following conversion, compared to the like three quarters before conversion. Undoubtedly, the open agency burdens

EXHIBIT 6–12
Lapse Rates before and after Conversion
(Conversion Date: April 1964)

	Account Business		Notice Business	
	First-Year Net Lapse	Total Net Lapse	First-Year Net Lapse	Total Net Lapse
Branch 7				
March 1963	0.107	2.147	0.042	1.793
September 1963	0.092	2.233	0.056	1.676
March 1964	0.130	2.741	0.100	1.958
September 1964	0.091	1.949	0.054	1.446
December 1964	0.077	1.343	0.051	1.577
Branch 8				
March 1963	0.115	2.270	0.042	1.530
September 1963	0.120	2.670	0.061	1.800
March 1964	0.192	2.674	0.149	2.430
September 1964	0.118	2.034	0.114	2.231
December 1964	0.102	2.041	0.098	1.967

EXHIBIT 6–13
Comparison of Unit Performance and Regular Manager
Compensation Three Quarters after Conversion versus
Comparable Quarters in the Year before Conversion

Regular Manager	Percent Change in NPM 1 by Unit—Three Quarters After Conversion versus Comparable Quarters Before Conversion	Percent Change in Regular Manager Compensation Three Quarters after Conversion Versus Comparable Quarters Before Conversion
7A	10.3*	1.9
7B	(6.4) *	nc§
8A	(44.0) †	(0.8)
8B	(7.5) †	nc

( )Denotes decrease.
*Data unavailable for one of the ten agencies.
†Data unavailable for two of the nine agencies.
§nc = virtually no change.
Note: For a detailed analysis by agency, see Appendix IV.

suffered in branch 8 are reflected in the poor showing of regular manager 8A especially. The inference made above about the cumulating pressure felt by a regular manager whose behavior significantly deviates from the proposed pattern proved true in the case of regular manager 8A. Before the beginning of the fourth quarter after conversion he asked to be "demoted" to agency status—a big step after almost three decades as first-line supervisor. Note again that the new compensation formula did not proportionally sanction the ineffective manager initially.

SUMMARY

The postconversion behavior of the first-line supervisors in branches 1 through 8 showed that the consultant's conversion process had gone far in moving the first-line supervisors from their preconversion behavior to the proposed behavior. In large measure their activities, interactions, and sentiments shifted in the proposed direction—that of behaving like decentralized line managers. However, there were deviations—in all likelihood transitional—that appeared in the research data. These deviations are summarized below. (An analysis, relating these deviations to the conversion process employed by the consultant, will be presented in the following chapter.)

Outstanding among the deviations in activity pattern was the tendency of the first-line supervisor to continue "demonstration selling" instead of introducing "clinical or field training" with his agents. Few actually did the proposed training. As a matter of fact, field time was eroded for most first-line supervisors by in-office activity, often consuming double the time that was proposed. The new involvement in the information flow system and the novel privacy of an office seemed to keep the first-line supervisor desk-bound. Despite the time spent in "paper shuffling," the first-line supervisor generally did not do as much planning in his agent and branch manager conferences as was proposed. Finally, the nonprogrammed activities surrounding termination and agent disability seemed more disruptive than anticipated. The first-line supervisor found it very difficult to work himself out of a hole now that he had continuing responsibility for a unit of agents.

The interaction pattern deviations seemed less serious than those in the activity pattern, though the office detail often did cause him to be alone more than double the time proposed. His penchant for "demonstration selling" and checking or controlling rather than planning did lead him to initiate more in his contacts with agents than proposed. Therefore, he was too dominant with subordinates, while still remaining in too much of a responder role with his superior.

In sentiment there was a minority, about equally divided in feeling, that they were dominated by the branch manager or were abandoned by the branch manager. After a "honeymoon" period in the new position, many first-line supervisors experienced some doubts about the career attractiveness of their jobs. They became quite sensitive to the competition among regular managers themselves and between regular managers and special managers—the latter were supposedly their organizational peers but enjoyed some differentiating advantages. This new competitiveness within a branch reflected the provincialism that many first-line supervisors felt concerning their own agency unit, instead of the balance of branch and unit spirit hoped for by the consultant.

Measurable performance indices supported the contention that the consultant had achieved relative success in improving business results through a behavioral change, especially among first-line supervisors. Lapse control generally improved, as did expense control. In the critically important generation of net new premiums, the performance measures indicated an overall improvement, but such improvement lagged the first-line supervisor's behavioral change.

This completes the analytic description of the case study—preconversion behavior and the forces shaping it, proposed behavior pattern and the plans to effect the change, and postconversion behavior. In the next two chapters, there is a distillation of more general concepts about the management of organizational change from this case study: first some thoughts on the theory of planning change, then some thoughts on the theory of controlling the change process during transition.

CHAPTER SEVEN

Conclusions—The Planning of Change

INTRODUCTION

REGULAR MANAGER postconversion behavior is substantially different from assistant manager preconversion behavior. Behavior has changed in the direction of the proposed behavior pattern, but the consultant's plans have not been so effective up to the time of this research as to have achieved the proposed pattern completely. It would be a mistake to imply that this is an evaluation of a *fait accompli*. The consultant did not simply design a system, plan its installation, and then leave. In a continuing client-consultant relationship, the parties in concert frequently refine the system itself, its installation procedure, and its administration. This research includes the refinements made up to the point of the study's completion in September 1964. These refinements were insignificant enough that the researcher could feel confident about evaluating an identifiable set of plans for effecting change. In evaluating the planning of this change two approaches will be taken. First, we will seek to explain the relative success of the consultant's plans in light of the relatively new and conflicting theoretical insights about organizational change from the social sciences. Second, we will examine the major deviations between the postconversion and proposed behavior patterns and relate them to the plans designed to effect the change. After this analysis of the clinical data, we will conceptualize in a more general way about effective planning for organizational change.

REASONS FOR THE RELATIVE SUCCESS OF THE PLANNED CHANGE

Understanding the basic conversion policies and the plans for information and exhortation, supervised learning by doing and sys-

temic alterations will require a prior analysis of the more fundamental issues of the consultant's role, focus, and intervention
strategy. These three facets of the client-consultant relationship are
tantamount to planning premises and hence must be explored before
a specific evaluation of the plans that directly affect the regular
manager.

Role, Focus, and Intervention Strategy

As pointed out in Chapter One, the change agent in much of
organization change effort where social scientists are involved plays
a very collaborative role. Recall that Warren Bennis refers to "researchers, trainers, consultants, teachers, and counselors."[1] None of
these role definitions adequately defines the consultant's basic
posture in this case. On a collaborative-unilateral continuum, the
consultant in this case would be much closer to the unilateral end
of the scale than any of the roles identified by Bennis. Hence, a new
term must be introduced. If the word "engineer" had not assumed
such a pejorative colloquial connotation, it would be appropriate.
In its stead, the word "peritus"[2] will serve. Certainly, the consultant
at times wore the hats of the more collaborative roles identified by
Bennis, but the basic posture was peritus—one who determines *what*
should be done and *how* to do it.

Alvin Gouldner's article, "Engineering and Clinical Approaches
to Consulting,"[3] raises a related issue regarding the consultant's role
in this case. One of the distinguishing features between the engineer
and clinician roles he defines is the engineer's willingness to accept
the client's definition of the problems and the clinician's insistence
on doing his own diagnostic work to separate problem from symp-
tom. The consultant in this case, as is obvious from the change in
mandate early in the engagement, does not fit the Gouldner
engineering role in this respect. As a matter of fact, the peritus bears
little resemblance to Gouldner's "engineer," which seems more like
a parody on the stereotype "efficiency expert." The engineer-clinician
dichotomy is too polar, too black and white, to be a useful typology.

---

[1]Bennis, Warren G., "A New Role for the Behavioral Sciences: Effecting Organizational Change," *Administrative Science Quarterly* (September 1963), 142.

[2]"Peritus" is borrowed from the Latin (*perior*, to experience) and means an expert,
with knowledge derived from experience.

[3]Gouldner, Alvin W., "Explorations in Applied Social Science-Engineering and
Clinical Approaches to Consulting," *Social Problems*, III (No. 2, January 1956), 173–81.

In seeking to understand the consultant's role, it may be helpful to note how the consultant behaved in the early stages of the consulting engagement. Among the top management, the consultant utilized the power of fact (a thorough diagnosis and consultant-supervised pilot tests) and rational argument to gain a commitment for change—change in a predetermined direction. Some, though not all, of the top executives contributed to the data and its analysis. They were not mere data sources; they participated in response to the peritus in the prereport stage and especially during the formulation of the specific action program. In some cases the participation was objective as well as psychological—measurable contribution or influence compared to perceived influence.[4] Outside of the home office—in the branches, where we are chiefly concerned—participation in the system design did not occur. The 22 offices visited in the diagnostic phase were merely data sources. It should be noted, though, that the personnel in the first three pilot test branches, especially, played a fairly active role in refining and "debugging" the change program already designed by the consultant. However, branch management as a whole neither had, nor felt it had, any influence on the proposed changes. Early in the engagement the consultants did discuss the possibility of building up the proposed changes on the basis of the experience of the most successful branches rather than on their own theoretical knowledge and experience. This plan was not employed, however, except for the use of some insights about physical changes gained in visits to foreign branches of the insurance company where experiments were underway with a system something like the one the consultants proposed. In summary, then, in the design stage, the consultant as peritus used the authority of expertise with some client participation to gain commitment for change at the top of the organization. Enough of the key executives had a sense of participation so that they could identify with the consultant.

In effecting the change, after pilot-test demonstrations, the consultant stepped back and had the client's own operating executives "sell" the new system. At the branch level the new system was identified as a company product, not a foreign element introduced by outsiders. This approach at the branch level reflected a sensitive appreciation for the culture of the company. By using direct-line su-

---

[4]This distinction is used in The Foundation for Research on Human Behavior, *Managing Major Change in Organizations* (Ann Arbor, Michigan, 1961), 71.

periors, the regional managers, to introduce the new system, the consultant capitalized on the rather unique trust in top management that permeated the company. Despite the two recent incidents that had cast a shadow on this trust among the regular agents, there was a widespread acceptance for what management proposed—a wide zone of acceptance, in the classical management terms. Though the branch personnel did not have a sense of participation in the system design,[5] they generally did have this trust that "if the company says it will work, it will! If the company finds out the system doesn't work, it will change the system!" According to the model presented in *Managing Major Change in Large Organizations,*[6] acceptance of change is codetermined by the degree of perceived control of the environment and of the change and the degree of trust in the change initiators. In turn, this perceived control and trust vary with the extent of information about the change, the extent of psychological participation in the change, other factors like the degree of acceptance of organizational folklore, the history of change experiences in the organization, and personality. In this case the consultant's approach relied on the acceptance of organizational folklore and the prior good experiences with change in the organization (with the two exceptions mentioned in reference to the regular agents). Through the regional manager, the consultant did make an effort to inform all concerned about the change (the timing of this information will be questioned later). As the experience under the new system grew, testimonials from participants became a relatively important part of this information effort in the later conversions. Once the decision was made that successful branches would not be the model for the new system, the last opportunity for giving branch personnel a chance for a sense of participation—at least representative participation—was lost. Predictably, then, some resistance to change should have been expected—and was, by both consultant and client.

It should be clear from this description of the consultant's behavior that he certainly did not behave unilaterally with his client.

---

[5]The regular managers did get some sense of participation, however, in the implementation of the new system. It was their assigned task during the orientation session just prior to the conversion to assign the regular agents in the office to units equal in potential. In branch 7, for instance, the two regular managers had to assign the 20 regular agents to two units in such a way that the 2 regular managers would be willing to accept either unit as his in a draw. There was no other significant participation in the implementation stage involving any branch personnel.

[6]The Foundation for Research on Human Behavior, *op. cit.,* p. 69.

Yet the consultant did not collaborate in the sense implied by social scientist change agents.[7] From all evidence the consultant perceived himself as peritus and performed as the experienced expert who was expected to advise what to do and how to do it.

Did the peritus role fit this particular client situation? As was pointed out in the beginning of Chapter Five, there was a sense of urgency arising from a worsening competitive position. True, the original issue that brought client and consultant together was the rather narrow problem of branch management compensation. Quite quickly, however, this issue was seen as symptomatic of a much broader concern, and some members of the insurance company's top management felt a strong need to take action on a broader front— identifying a more appropriate market niche and organizing so as to position resources in that market niche. The consultant's sponsor within the insurance company, the senior vice president of sales management, felt most strongly about this. He had watched the internal committee work for almost a year on the narrow branch management compensation issue without significant results. It was evident that even if the senior vice president comprehended the whole organizational need, the management team itself could not shoulder the project effectively, given the time pressures from the sense of urgency. Also, given the very normal variations in perceptions and even values among the top executives, no one man could readily made the team gel. This in large measure accounts for the role expectations the consultant faced in his dealings with the senior vice president, the client sponsor. He was not simply looking for help in making management operate more effectively in a general sense. This was a goal-oriented project. The sponsor expected an expert who would say what to do and how. The consultant's credentials proved he could fit such role expectations. In consulting philosophy, the consultant envisioned his own role as a directive change agent, as active peritus. In the particular circumstances of this case—the role expectations of the sponsor feeling some urgency to accomplish a specific goal that seemed beyond the immediate competence of the management team—the consultant's use of the peritus role seems appropriate.

The consultant focused on the client company more as an ineffi-

---

[7]See the chapter "Influence without Authority: Collaborative Models" in Leavitt, Harold J., *Managerial Psychology* (Chicago, Ill.: The University of Chicago Press, 1964), 189–205.

cient technical system than as an ineffective social system. The consultant was not unaware that inhibited individuals and/or interpersonal incompetence might fault the operation of the system. As a matter of fact, the consultant demonstrated keen sensitivity to the social system in dealing with the top management group. It is the focus at the branch office level, however, that most interests us here. Because there were several hundred branch offices, the consultant would hardly focus on the specific social system of each branch. At best, the consultant could focus on a model branch social system, as he did with the model branch technical system. Abstracting this way to the model level, the consultant could not focus on the self-actualization of individuals or the interpersonal competence of group members. The focus had to be on a socio-*technical* system. Again, in the terminology of operations research, we might say the consultant was maximizing the efficiency of the technical system within the constraints of the social system. In this focus he was unlike those social scientists who seem to maximize the effectiveness of the social system within the constraints of the technical system. Personal values aside, the consultant in his change-agent role could hardly be said to add to his concern for economic efficiency the crusading spirit for democratic values felt by some social scientists, as pointed out by Bennis: "There is growing disenchantment with the moral neutrality of the scientist. . . . For social scientists and actionists, for example, the infusion of democratic values in bureaucratic institutions remains an unconquered promise."[8]

Given the entry conditions described above, the consultant's focus seems appropriate, especially in value emphasis. As will be seen later, the consultant's model of the branch office social system seems to have presumed more independence than was the case. In this sense, the focus on the branch technical system in which the units were independent may have obscured the social interdependence.

In the area of intervention strategy the consultant differed from the approach of most of the social scientists working on planned change. Of course, the choice of role and focus predetermines much of the intervention strategy. Rather than attempt to educe behavioral change at the first-line supervisor level by directly changing the knowledge and/or attitudes of the branch office personnel with group dynamics techniques like sensitivity training, the consultant

---

[8]Bennis, *op. cit.*, pp. 128–29.

chose to "engineer" the external forces which molded first-line supervisor behavior. Schein seems to call it "compliance" when "the
individual . . . changes because he is *forced* to change by the agent's
direct manipulation of rewards and punishments . . ."[9] In his systemic alterations the consultant did indeed "manipulate" rewards
and punishments as part of a larger strategy of altering the whole
structure shaping the role demands for the first-line supervisor. In a
sense, then, it was compliance rather than "conversion" (as Leonard
Sayles[10] uses the term to apply to behavior change brought on by
cognitive or attitude change) the first-line supervisor displayed in
his new role as a line manager.

The consultant did perceive the information and exhortation
program and the supervised learning-by-doing program as integral
to his intervention strategy. As will be seen later in this chapter,
these efforts were in fact of relatively minor consequence. Had these
two programs been designed and conducted differently, the intervention strategy as a whole would have taken on the character of a
"conversion" effort.

Could what Leonard Sayles calls a "conversion approach"—action
research, sensitivity training, the management grid technique and
the like—have effected the necessary change? This obviously must remain an open question. Two points favor the intervention strategy
used by the consultants in this case. Social scientists involved in other
intervention strategies admit that their approaches have worked
best where the goal orientation was relatively nonspecific (changing
values, increasing interpersonal competence, etc.). Here the goal
was quite specific: position resources in the best market niche.
Second, the techniques employed by these social scientists, to this
point at least, have involved long periods of time. In sensitivity
training, for instance, "Blake and his colleagues estimate the time
required for the first four phases—appreciation sessions, team training, horizontal linking, and setting of organizational goals—may be
two years or longer. Implementing them may require an additional
two years."[11] In the case at hand it was barely a year from the beginning of the engagement to the conversion of the first branch (see

---

[9]Schein, Edgar H., "Management Development as a Process of Influence," *Industrial Management Review*, II, 2, May, 1961.

[10]Sayles, Leonard R., "The Change Process in Organizations: An Applied Anthropology Analysis," *Human Organization*, XXI, No. 2 (Summer 1962), 66.

[11]Bennis, *op. cit.*, p. 152.

the timetable in Appendix II. Even at that, there was rather intense pressure "to get rolling." The "conversionists" might argue that their approaches produce more lasting benefits to the executive team in terms of their ability to cope with their roles in the future. The evidence here is inconclusive, and some of the social scientists express a concern, as in this quote from Argyris cited by Bennis:

> The fade-out phenomenon is a crucial one. I agree that fade-out will be expected . . . if organization structure, etc., are not modified. However, I also expect fade-out because openness, trust, etc., cannot be delegated, transferred from one group to another. It has to be earned.[12]

Only with the foregoing analysis of the role, focus, and intervention strategy—the planning premises, as it were—can we proceed with the inquiry into the relative effectiveness of the conversion policies and plans themselves.

Basic Conversion Policies

The five basic conversion policies listed in Chapter Five proved to be critical in the planning of change. In part, they are responsible for the relative success of the planned change, but they also contributed to some of the difficulties. The first two policies grew out of the consultant's role perception and have been already mentioned in that context, so only a brief word on each is needed here. The last three policies are a product of the consultant's sensitivity to the company's manpower resource constraint—admittedly more compromises with the facts of life than optimal policies in a theoretical sense.

First, in using the pilot test approach as part of the rational argumentation to top management, the consultant was able to give on-the-line training to those company executives who would later shoulder the burden of coordinating the nationwide conversion effort. The vice president conversion coordinator was involved from the beginning. The man who was to become his senior lieutenant held a branch manager position in one of the first three pilot test branches. This continuity of trained leadership made consultant withdrawal from the conversion effort, after heavy involvement in the pilot tests, a workable policy.

Second, the consultant passed on his change-agent role in the im-

---

[12]*Ibid.*, note 94, p. 159.

plementation stage to the newly appointed regional managers. This policy of putting the change in the hands of the direct line managers reflected both an effort to avoid any retreat to the former central staff control and an eagerness to make the implementation effort consistent with the managerial philosophy of the new system. Other than the staff back-up provided from the home office by the conversion coordination unit and the temporary staff help of an assistant regional manager, the purity of the system was preserved. In his role as change agent the regional manager served as a model for his branch and regular managers. Not only could superior and subordinates get to know one another as they could no other way, but the regional manager could set the example for managing within the philosophy of the new system. The four days of the orientation sessions just prior to the conversion of each branch provided the best, though brief, opportunity for this learning experience.

Third, the decision was made to install the new system full blown in each branch, without any phasing of programmed steps. No branch personnel would receive the "Guides" for the new positions until just before the preconversion orientation. Also, neither systemic alterations nor behavioral modifications were to be made officially until the time of conversion. Since the fourth basic policy set a conversion timetable of four branches per region per quarter as each new regional manager was appointed and trained, it would take more than three years to complete the conversion process. While branches awaited their turn for conversion, they were guided by no formal policy on how to prepare—or whether to prepare at all —for the forthcoming change. Efforts to give the assistant managers expanded roles in the conduct of the general branch meetings received official sanction, but any efforts to assign assistant managers their own equal staffs or to change the agent reporting days generally met disapproval. The fear was that added confusion might result if branch personnel had to go through radical changes twice in such a brief period. Nonetheless, such preparatory steps were being made in some branches, as they were to some degree in branches 7 and 8. Without the official "Guides" there was no assurance that such steps would be functional preparation. Secondhand information about the new system could leave room for misconceptions, as it did in branches 7 and 8 (one branch in the same metropolitan area and another within 30 miles were converted before branches 7 and 8). Recall that in the model for predicting the degree of resistance to change (see footnote 6) information about the change becomes relatively more important if there is little or no sense of participation—as was the case in the branches. By reserving to the regional manager the function of communicating the detailed "package" officially at the time of each branch's conversion, room was left for the build-up of resistance to the change even before the change reached a particular branch.

The fourth basic conversion policy is important for another reason. Since the regional manager was to convert each of his 20 or more branches himself on a four-per-quarter basis after converting one bellwether branch in the first quarter, the greater share of the first two years in his new position would be spent in this activity. Only when his conversion cycle was over could he effectively fill the regional manager position as originally designed. Only when the scheduled activities of the change-agent role were complete could the regional manager personally supervise all his branches and allocate his time on a priority basis to those branches needing the most help.

This initial double role for the regional manager becomes even more important in light of the fifth basic conversion policy. Though training programs were being planned for branch and regular managers, the decision was made to introduce the new system to the pilot-test branches without formal training in the new duties. When the national conversion was begun in March 1963, the training materials and program were still in the development stage, so the conversion process contained no provision for branch manager or regular manager training. As this research ended, training of selected regular managers had begun in a couple of regions. This training in selected areas, like recruiting, came after the regular managers had operated under the new system for some time. Also, all newly appointed regular managers received special training in the home office in the duties of the newly defined position. Plans for specially training branch managers after, if not before, conversion were still in the formulation stage as this research ended. What makes this point so important is the consultant's finding in the diagnostic phase of the engagement recorded in the report outlined in Appendix II:

Although well trained in selling skills, managers receive little training in *how to manage* before taking over a branch . . . . Once on a job, most managers get very little coaching on *how to manage.* . . . result of this limited on-the-job training: some managers learn by doing; many others never learn to plan or manage effectively . . . . Conclusion: underlying any strengthening of branch management is the need to step up the training and direction of managers in how to run a successful branch.

Without formal training before, or as part of, the conversion process, heavy reliance is placed on the other elements in the process of planned change: the information and exhortation program, the supervised learning-by-doing program, and the program of systemic alterations. The regional manager, occupied as he is with the conversion schedule—through especially the first two of these three programmed elements of the planned change—must compensate for the absence of the much-needed formal training.

Key Elements in the Plans to Effect the Change

In looking for the reasons for the relative success of the planned change, we could not ignore the planning premises nor the basic conversion policies, but of major importance are those phases of the planned change process that directly "touched" the regular manager. The degree of success in moving the regular manager from his pre-conversion behavior pattern to the proposed behavior pattern depends on the information and exhortation program, the supervised learning-by-doing program, and particularly the program of systemic alterations.

For the regular manager, the information and exhortation program turns out to be a unique experience telescoped into two days immediately before the conversion date. In the presence of the regional manager, the assistant regional manager, and the branch manager and his peers, the regular manager hears the full explanation of *what* the changes entail and *why* the changes are being made. He sees a filmstrip and slide presentations; he participates in reading aloud from the "Guide"; he hears commentary from an enthused regional manager; he gets straightforward answers to his questions. The facts about the new position are so cogent that there is little difficulty in "selling" a regular manager on the new system. Regular manager 8C began the two days in a fighting mood (misconceptions based on misinformation), but halfway through the first day he was enthusiastically "on the bandwagon." The knottier problem is communicating a mass of information so as to get a satisfactory level of understanding. The regular managers in branches 7 and 8 felt "snowed" but had a sense of security in knowing "it's all in the

Guide."[13] This orientation session, dedicated to the *what* and *why,* was supplemented by a later skull session and practice session in the mechanics—the *how*—of the new branch marketing plan. *How* material on the rest of the regular manager's function appeared in the "patterns" section of his "Guide," which was read and commented on during the 2-day orientation. Note how sensitively these "patterns" are introduced:

The patterns which follow are a series of guidelines on How to Go About the Regular Manager's Job on a Day-to-Day Basis. These patterns are based on a set of time-tested principles for effective management—the basic aim of all Managers under the Line Management System of organization. Thus, they represent approaches which, in general, will lead to the best long term results.

These patterns are guide lines, not procedures. They must be applied with judgment by the Regular Managers. Since they are not procedures, they are not justification in themselves for ineffective performance even when followed exactly.

Nevertheless, the fundamental principles used in these patterns are so well acecpted that it will be a rare Regular Manager who can operate in ways that differ substantially from the methods described there and succeed over the long term. Inevitably the ultimate success of the Regular Manager will be tied to how well he is able to build increasingly capable and more highly motivated agents and, through them, to achieve better end results.

NOTE: These patterns are not written to be self-explanatory. This is because management methods—unlike routine procedures—cannot be reduced to mechanical steps. Consequently, these patterns will be meaningful primarily to those who have participated in detailed training discussions prior to their introduction.

As thorough and competent as the regional manager-led discussions were and as sophisticated and lucid as the "Guides" were (the researcher has found no better application of classical management theory in the literature), the regular manager could hardly have bridged the gap between intellectual appreciation and skill development during the orientation session. The information and exhortation program achieved an adequate, and even better than adequate, understanding of *what* and *why*. In the absence of formal train-

---

[13]The fact that the researcher, despite months of exposure to the new system on paper and in operation, learned something new from both the branch 7 and the branch 8 orientation sessions may not be inappropriate commentary on this point.

ing, skill development in *how* depended on the program of supervised learning by doing.

The key to the regular manager's supervised learning by doing is the branch manager. Recall, however, that branch managers, who were not the most skilled managers under the old system, now had to cope with a new job, too. They had to gain skills in managing managers instead of salesmen, so even the branch manager who had a satisfactory level of managerial skills under the old system faced a new system requiring somewhat different skills. The branch manager himself was learning by doing. Unfortunately, his learning by doing could not be effectively supervised by his immediate superior. The regional manager, during the critical first two years under the new system, was occupied chiefly with his role as change agent in a rather tight conversion schedule. Below is the instruction from the regional manager's guide on this postconversion function.

The Regional Manager or the Assistant to the Regional Manager, or both together, should make at least three follow-up visits to the branch office in the six months following conversion. (This is a *minimum;* many branches, where management experiences difficulty in changing working habits and attitudes, will require more frequent visits.) The purpose of these visits will be to answer questions that may have arisen concerning the new system but, more importantly, to make certain that members of branch management are adopting patterns of operation that are consistent with the new system.

Because it is so important that the new system get off on the right foot in each branch the first follow-up visit should be made within the first month following the conversion date.

During the course of each follow-up visit, the Regional Manager and Assistant to the Regional Manager should make it a point to talk with all of the Regular and Special Managers and with a number of the Regular and Special Agents in order to get a first-hand impression of the current state of morale and attitudes toward the new system in the branch.

Since the prime purpose of these visits is to see that management is developing skill in carrying out important activities under the new system, most of the discussion with the Branch Manager should be focused on assessing the progress of the Regular and Special Managers. To stimulate the Branch Manager' thinking and to provide a basis for discussion, the Branch Manager should be asked to complete the Inventory of Key Management Skills using the Regular and Special Manager Rating Guides prior to the visit.

These ratings and the reasons for them should be discussed in detail and a specific action plan for helping each man develop the skills he needs should be drawn up by the Branch Manager. This action plan, even though it might be extremely simple, should be committed to writing to serve as a basis for checking progress at the time of the next visit.

In addition, when a Regional Manager is making the visit, he should assess the progress of the Branch Manager himself. The following are some points to consider in this assessment:

Weekly conferences with Regular and Special Managers . . .
Training Regular and Special Managers . . .
Maintenance of branch morale . . .

The recommended follow-up visits are made—sometimes by the assistant regional manager alone—but both regional and branch managers tend to agree that such time is generally spent "fire fighting" or problem solving. These visits scarcely focused on supervised skill development. After the six-month period branch managers could, and in branches 1 to 6 did, have no personal supervision for six months or more at a time.[14] If the branch manager's own skill development did not progress, the regular manager could hardy expect the most fruitful experience in his supervised learning-by-doing program. Skill development became in many cases an inefficient trial-and-error process. This situation was alleviated somewhat because the "environment" of the regular managers was so engineered by the systemic alterations that errors from this trial-and-error process brought sanctions, in the long run at least. Given these systemic alterations, a regular manager could not "comfortably" deviate very far from the proposed behavior pattern for very long.

Inherent in the use of the systemic alterations to effect a new behavior pattern there would seem to be implicit assumptions akin to the Watsonian behavioral or stimulus-response model.

Stimulus ⟶ [   ] ⟶ Response

To elicit a different response, one must introduce a different stimulus. The "black box" responding to the stimulus may be an individual or a group. In the pure application of the stimulus-response model, no approach is made directly to the "black box"; no direct

---

[14]Just as this research was being completed, the company instructed each of its regional managers to spend about three consecutive days in each of his branches after he completed the conversion of all branches. This period was to be used for a depth analysis and evaluation of the branches' operation under line management.

appeal is made to intellect or emotions by rational persuasion or influence. An analogy that comes to mind concerning a nonhuman system is the Pavlovian-type experiments in "rat psychology." In the change effort under study here the desired response is the proposed behavior pattern; the "black box" represents the regular manager. The authority structure, the reward structure, the work-flow system, the information-flow system, and the physical structure make up the relevant stimuli to be "engineered" in eliciting the new response. Virtually all the "signals" the regular manager receives from his structural environment were changed. Of course, the consultant did not only employ systemic alterations in his planned change effort. He used information and exhortation as well as supervised learning by doing. Consequently, his was not a pure application of the stimulus-response model. There was an attempt to influence directly the regular manager, the "black box," in addition to the efforts at engineering the world around the regular manager, the stimuli.[15] Sayles holds that this multiple approach is a prerequisite for effective organizational change.

It should now be evident that the applied anthropologist's theory of change and administration encompasses both traditional methods of persuasion and influence, usually emphasized in social psychological terms but operationally definable in behavioral, interaction terms, and more long-run or permanent alterations in the organizational constraints. In another work we have chosen to call the former "conversion" by which we meant simply that the manager seeks to convince or persuade a subordinate to shift his behavior in some way and thus eliminate a source of disturbance.

Obviously, this type of administrative activity is important and constantly used. It is involved in the giving of brief orders and lengthy disciplinarian sessions. But the administrator who relies solely on this type of change is ignoring one of the most important parts of his job: seeking out and remedying the persisting and compounding problems. These require, as we have endeavored to illustrate, the introduction of changes in the organi-

---

[15]March and Simon adopt such a learning model in their book, *Organizations*, which emphasizes the importance of the environment: "The behavior of an organism through a short interval of time is to be accounted for by (1) its internal state at the beginning of the interval, and (2) its environment at the beginning of the interval. The same two sets of factors, the initial state and the environment, determine not only the behavior but also what the internal state will be at the next moment of time." [March, James G., and Simon, Herbert A., *Organizations* (New York: John Wiley & Sons, Inc., 1959), 9.] Leavitt, too, assigns an important causal role in behavior to the stimuli outside the individual. [Leavitt, Harold J., *Managerial Psychology* (Chicago: University of Chicago Press, 1964), 9.]

zational constraints: the flow of work, the components of jobs, the incumbents on jobs, the structure of authority, the incentives and even the controls themselves that are used.[16]

In engineering these structural constraints on the regular manager's position, further assumptions are made. Following the theoretical orientation of Kurt Lewin, organizational behavior may be viewed as a process maintained by dynamic equilibrium by a balanced field of forces:[17]

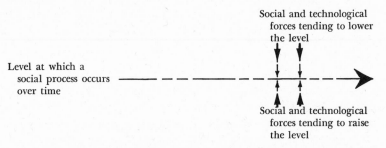

Note: the number and length of the arrows is roughly a reflection of the number and strength of the forces at that point.

In engineering the structural constraints, the forces controlling the behavior pattern of the regular manager, the consultant presumably must know the following:

1. What these forces are.
2. The relative strength of these forces.
3. The probable impact of substituting one force for another.
4. The probable time lag between alteration of a force and full impact on the system.

In a mechanical system one could apply physical laws and utilize laboratory experiments to become informed on these matters. In dealing with organic or holistic systems—an individual man, a group, or an organization—there is less assurance the change agent can be so fully informed. Great strides have been made in the psychiatric relationship. The action researchers or sensitivity trainers have begun fruitful work with group situations. However, in dealing with several hundred group situations in an abstracted model of the branch office

16Sayles, *op. cit.*, p. 66.

17The Foundation for Research on Human Behavior, *op. cit.*, p. 62 ff. The model is drawn from Lewin's "Studies in Group Decisions," in *Group Dynamics: Research and Theory*, eds. Cartwright, D., and Zander, A. (Evanston, Ill.: Row, Peterson & Co., 1953).

socio-technical system, the consultant was restricted to a lower order knowledge about the relevant variables. Realizing that each branch varied—that the field of forces would not be exactly the same in each—the consultant had to rely on a diagnosis of a sample of the branches and on his general experience and theoretical insights. One would expect, too, that in this situation the consultant might over-engineer some of the forces, at least as regards particular branches, if not for all branches.

Not knowing which are the key forces, it is advisable to alter more specific forces than are actually required to compensate for our inadequate knowledge. This kind of planned and careful overdetermination means working with more social and technological forces than may at first seem necessary to change an event. While mobilizing extra forces may require an added expenditure of energy and time, the advantage to be gained is in an increase in the probability that change will occur in the direction desired. The balance or equilibrium which develops is usually quite stable. This is especially true if the social process is of importance to many parts of the organization. The more aspects of the work flow of the organization that the process affects, the greater the number of forces acting upon the system and tending to keep it functioning at its present level.[18]

Also, given the consultant's particular expertise in, and focus on, the technical aspects of the socio-technical system, we might expect greater sensitivity in the engineering of the technical rather than the social forces.

Recall that while the environmental context (external and internal economics and the institutional setting) was a minor part of the basic influences on regular manager behavior, the consultant could not and did not try to engineer these environmental variables. More important, the behavioral context, too, influenced behavior. That is, the behavior patterns of the branch manager and the agents helped mold the regular manager's behavior pattern. The consultant did include the behavioral context among the forces shaping the regular manager's behavior, but he did not attempt to engineer the behavioral context directly. The behavior patterns of the branch manager and the agents were to be changed *at the same time,* and *by the same planned change process,* as the regular manager's—the information and exhortation program, the supervised learning-by-doing program, and the program of systemic alterations. However,

---

[18]The Foundation for Research on Human Behavior, *op. cit.,* p. 64.

from the point of view of effecting change in the regular manager's behavior pattern, it would seem that prior consideration could well have been given to the changing of the branch manager segment of the behavioral context. Obviously, in the best of all worlds, the entire field of forces influencing regular manager behavior—systemic as well as behavioral context—should have been engineered prior to the effort to change regular manager behavior. However, the same thing could be said for the branch manager and for the agent, in which cases the regular manager's behavior would be part of the field of forces to be engineered in advance. In the approach taken by the consultant there was no planned priority in effecting changes at any level of the behavioral context. Yet the design of the new system implicitly assumes that a subordinate's adoption of a new behavior pattern would be facilitated by the revised behavior pattern of his superior. A changed behavior pattern at the branch manager level is a necessary condition (but not a necessary and sufficient condition) for the change in behavior pattern of all but the exceptional regular manager.

This theoretical treatment of the relative effectiveness of the consultant's plans for achieving the proposed regular manager behavior pattern can be summarized as follows:

1. The consultant's chosen role as peritus did not directly affect the regular manager, except insofar as it "got the ball rolling" in circumstances where company resources otherwise could not have been marshalled effectively, given the time pressure. Since there was almost no branch participation in the system design and limited participation in system implementation, great reliance was placed on the regular manager's trust in the company and on the effectiveness of the information and exhortation program.

2. The consultant's focus on the technical and economic aspects of the socio-technical branch system more so than on the individual, interpersonal, or human values aspects burdened the branch personnel with the task of accommodating to the change as an interdependent social unit.

3. The intervention strategy, aimed at producing "compliance" more than "conversion," seems responsive to the entry conditions, especially the time pressure. It remains moot whether long run effects were sacrificed for short run expediency.

4. The basic conversion policies, passing the role of change agent to the regional manager, capitalized on the regular manager's identification with the company. However, the timing decision, giving the regional manager such a busy conversion schedule, and the decision to use no formal training as part of the conversion process set the stage for a prolonged transition to the proposed regular manager behavior pattern. The information and exhortation program, while it communicated the *what* and the *why,* could only provide an intellectual appreciation of the *how,* not true skill development.

5. Skill development for the regular manager was retarded because the branch manager's learning by doing was virtually unsupervised (the regional manager was busy with his conversion schedule) and therefore could not be an effective mentor in the regular manager's learning by doing.

6. Since there was no prior attention to changing the branch manager's behavior pattern, the total field of forces determining the regular manager's behavior pattern was not under control. Hence, transitionally regular manager behavior at times did not stay "on track" to the proposed pattern.

7. The engineering of the systemic variables turned out to be the most important aspect of the consultant's plans. The regular manager's structural environment was so altered that he could not deviate too far and too long from the proposed pattern.

It remains now to relate the most significant transitional problems —where the regular manager deviated most from the proposed pattern—to the consultant's plans for effecting the change.

MAJOR DEVIATIONS AND THE CONSULTANT'S PLANS

In comparing the postconversion behavior in Chapter Six with the proposed behavior in Chapter Five, certain deviations appear. Above we focused on the plans in an effort to explain their relative effectiveness. It became clear that the plans could indeed go far in effecting change, but they left room for at least some transitional deviations. In this section the viewpoint turns to these transitional deviations, and an effort is made to show what aspects of the plans are accountable for the major gaps between the postconversion and the proposed behavior pattern.

Deviations in Activities

Most regular managers spend less time in clinical or field activities with agents than proposed. In the normal workweek, "paper shuffling" increased the in-office activity time. The systemic alterations in the schedule brought him to the office more often than under the former system. The new involvement in the information-flow system required the handling of an unaccustomed volume of "paper," and the office layout changes gave him the unaccustomed privacy of an office. These were just conditions occasioning more office time. The cause in most instances was a lack of diagnostic skills. Much time was spent in reviewing reports and rearranging recorded facts without much consequent action in the areas of planning or control. The branch manager had little or no more facility with the new information flow than the regular manager, and he was finding difficulty in letting go of his former habits of information processing and record keeping. Consequently, the regular manager often did not have helpful, supervised learning by doing.

Field or clinical time with agents was even more dramatically cut in the nonnormal workweeks, when the regular manager was burdened with one or more open agencies. This situation is a fact of life in the insurance industry, but it had an unexpected impact on the branch during transition. In the cases of single and especially multiple open agencies, the regular manager had a particularly difficult time "digging out" and getting back into the field with his agents. In the branches visited, open agencies stayed open longer than under the old system. As pointed out earlier, a regular manager could quite easily get involved in a vicious circle—a second agent might leave because the regular manager was too busy caring for an open agency to properly service his other agents. Several aspects of the consultant's plans contribute to this problem. First, the new authority system made a fixed unit of agents the sole responsibility of one regular manager. Second, the changes in the reward system put the regular managers "in business for themselves." Each was financially independent for about 85 percent of his income, drawing only about 15 percent from a common pool. It was literally true that "you had to hurt yourself to help a brother regular manager." Third, in the authority system the branch manager was left with the initiative of declaring an emergency and assigning one man to help another. In the process of adjusting to the role of delegator, most branch managers were more conscious of "stepping back" than of exercising judgment in initiating emergency assistance. Finally, the regular manager had been delegated the responsibility for doing his own recruiting but had no specific opportunity for skill development. In their eagerness to "step back," most branch managers seemed to confuse the need to truly delegate the function and the need to train the regular managers in the function—a training task most branch managers could do competently. In short, the regular manager did not have the skill to cope with a situation in which the new system left him very much alone.

While it was true that the character of the activity the regular manager engaged in during field assignments more resembled "demonstration selling" than more farsighted training, this concerned client and consultant to a lesser degree. It was realized that the regular manager could best win over the agents on his new unit by doing what he knew best, selling insurance. Besides, there was some hope that such selling activity would help to offset the expected transitional slump in sales due to the distraction of the conversion process. It seems, however, that after six quarters the shift to a training focus would have been more evident than it was in offices 1 to 6. Part of the explanation again seemed to be that the regular manager had not yet developed the new training skills necessary for the task. More important, though, was the strong expectation that persisted among agents that the new system would mean the regular manager would help them more—that is, sell for them more. Somehow, in the information and exhortation effort among agents the facts became clouded in the "sales pitch." The agent was promised more personal attention along with a more professional office environment, but he failed to get the message that the regular manager would necessarily have less time to allocate to field activities and that the character of field assignment activity would change. Consequently, agents put pressure on regular managers to sell, a pressure few found they could avoid.

Finally, the activity in the individual conferences did not include the hoped-for degree of forward planning. Where appropriate planning occurred, the regular manager showed diagnostic skills in handling records and reports. Generally, as has been said, such skills were lacking. In branches 2 and 4, however, where the branch managers spent the majority of individual conference time with their regular managers in planning, those same regular managers tended to provide the same experience for their agents. Since branch managers almost never observed individual conferences with agents, the supervised learning-by-doing experience became one of emulation of how the branch manager conducted his own individual conferences. It was generally a safe prediction that if the branch manager spent conference time largely on supervisory checks, the regular manager would behave comparably with his agents. This fact supports the earlier contention that there might well have been some phasing of the conversion or some priority given the effort to alter the branch manager's behavior.

Deviations in Interactions

What has been said above about deviations in activities explains most of the deviations in interactions—the reduced total time with individual agents and the preponderance of regular manager initiations in contacts with agents. "Demonstration selling" and supervisory checking require the regular managers to dominate initiations. There has been no mention yet of unit conferences. Postconversion behavior here conforms more closely to the proposed pattern than in individual conferences. However, many regular managers tend to dominate initiations and prevent the dialogue for which the room and group size are so conducive. It is natural for the regular manager to imitate the manner in which his branch manager used to conduct the larger general meetings. Most regular managers recognize that the "meeting method" is inappropriate for the purposes of the conferences in the new system, but there is no new model to emulate. For instance, there is no official provision for management conferences where the regular manager can see the branch manager demonstrating the appropriate techniques. Even if the branch manager observes a unit conference or conducts management conferences, he has no experience with conferences to draw on directly in training his regular managers, and he receives no supervised practice from the regional manager. Here is a case where the systemic alteration—the new professionally appointed conference room and the smaller unit—facilitates the adoption of the proposed pattern and, in fact, produces discomfort if the "meeting method" is used. Finally, the increased total interaction time with the branch manager—with the branch manager dominating the initiations—reflects situations where the branch manager seems overinvolved in details of specific policies, prospects, lapses, and the like or too preoccupied with supervisory checks. Some unprogrammed contacts would be expected, however.

Deviations in Sentiments

In only a minority of cases was the regular manager prevented from feeling like "the boss" by a branch manager who refused to "step back" and make the appropriate delegation. Almost as much of a deviation was the attitude among some regular managers that they were too much on their own, that more abdication than delegation had taken place. This happened in branch 8 and in those circumstances where regular managers would have preferred some assistance with open agency situations. This again is a case that argues for some prior attention to conversion of branch manager behavior or at least closer supervision from the regional manager.

The systemic alteration in compensation seemed to push the regular manager too far in a concern for conservation compared to production. Here was a case of overengineering the systemic variable and creating a gap between the needs of the agent and the regular manager. (A new agent contract now partially alleviates this situation.)

Initially, the regular manager found increased career attractiveness in the new position but, after the honeymoon effect created by the new title, the new office, and the seemingly better financial rewards, he became sensitive to a threat to his relative status. The special manager, formerly a peer to the regular manager in every sense, enjoyed a 25 percent salary differential, had direct access to clerical help and seemed to have higher earning potential without the hazard of open agency disturbances. In addition, the regular manager saw special agents on the special manager's unit enjoying private or semiprivate offices and phones, whereas even regular agents with better production records had to work with a common worktable and a drawer in a file cabinet. All of these were systemic alterations made by the consultant. It was not so much that the consultant's focus on the technical and economic aspects of the branch system blinded him to the social implications of the systemic changes—some "static" was predicted and was accepted as a calculated risk. The strength of this negative sentiment about changes in relative status seemed to be growing rather than diminishing during the transition.

Finally, the hoped-for balance of unit and branch allegiance was very slow in developing. As was pointed out above, the new compensation arrangements fostered an independent spirit and even a competitive spirit between regular managers that had not existed before. Quite often assistant managers formed a peer group under the old system. The new schedule and unit organization took away the opportunity to be together, just as it did with agent peer groups. There was no programmed interaction at all among regular managers under the new system. True, for operational purposes the units were independent, but they were competing for insurance sales in the same community and for manpower replacements. They became interdependent only in the cases of emergency. The spirit of all the alterations—except the common branch pool that contributed about 15 percent to each regular manager's total income—was independence or individualism. It is not surprising, then, even in emergency, that spontaneous management team spirit is not prevalent. It seems fair to judge that the consultant's engineering of the technical elements in the total field of forces determining regular manager behavior caused the balance to slip too far in one direction. After a prolonged transition, branch personnel accommodated the system— by introducing management meetings—to restore a cooperative spirit.

IMPLICATIONS FOR THE THEORY OF PLANNED CHANGE[19]

As indicated in Chapter One, recent developments in the field of organization change have been confined to a narrow range of collaborative, human-value-oriented, "conversion" approaches. Without a doubt, progress has been substantial, if somewhat unbalanced. The following implications from this case study hopefully will contribute to further and more balanced developments in our understanding about effective planning of organization change.

Entry conditions determine the appropriateness of the change-agent's role and intervention strategy. Given the specificity of the goal, the urgency of the felt need, the limitations of client resources, and the role expectation of the client, the change process would probably not have moved along so expeditiously without the peritus role and the "compliance" intervention strategies used. Certainly, other variables, which could be listed under the rubric "entry condi-

---

[19]See Appendix V for a technical note concerning the nature of the implications and the limitations to their applicability.

tions," influence the choice of role and intervention strategy: factors reflecting client sponsor and consultant personalities, ideologies, and competence, as well as situational factors like the relative sophistication of the technology, the need for secrecy, and so forth. (In a sense this issue is analogous to the factors influencing the choice of leadership style, so well discussed by Tannenbaum and Schmidt.[20]) However, the concurrence of the four factors—the specificity of the goal, the urgency of the felt need, the limitations of client resources, and the role expectation of the client—that the consultant so often faces seem to dictate the sort of approach used in this case. It is as inappropriate to choose a role and an intervention strategy on a value premise as it is to adopt either an autocratic or democratic leadership style for all situations on *a priori* criteria. The choice is pragmatic.[21]

In planning a change process, one would like to minimize the transition time between current behavior and proposed behavior. On the basis of this case study, certain factors seem critical in this effort to minimize the transition. First, where the behavioral change involves the acquisition of new skills, formal training and/or supervised learning by doing are necessary if a prolonged transition is to be avoided. This might seem so obvious as to be a truism, but often multiple levels in an organization are undergoing change, and implicit assumptions are made about the capacity of a superior, himself undergoing change, to supervise a subordinate's skill development. This point leads to our next observation.

Second, in engineering the total field of forces around an organizational position in order to change the behavior of the occupants of that position, prior attention will have to be given to parts of the behavioral context if a prolonged transition is to be avoided. Recall the use in this study of the categories "environmental," "structural," and "behavioral" to describe the field of forces molding behavior patterns in a particular position. The behavior patterns of superiors, peers, and subordinates make up the behavioral context for any particular position. A plan to simultaneously introduce a change at all levels seems to ignore the behavioral interdependencies such as the need for a mentor in the learning-by-doing process. One would

[20]Tannenbaum, Robert, and Schmidt, Warren H., "How to Choose a Leadership Pattern," *Harvard Business Review* (March-April 1958), 95–101.

[21]For a clear denial that laboratory training stands for some form of ideology see Schein, Edgar H., and Bennis, Warren G., *Personal and Organizational Change through Group Methods* (New York: John Wiley & Sons, 1965), 327–29.

have to expect a somewhat prolonged transition if the plan includes no sequencing of steps in the engineering of the total field of forces. Systemic alterations (in the authority structure, the reward system, the work-flow system, the information-flow system, and the physical structure), supported by an information and exhortation program, can induce a measure of immediate behavioral change and can serve as restraining forces, lest the behavioral changes get "off track." However, progress at each level toward the proposed behavior will be retarded somewhat, especially by the progress at the next higher level.

Third, in seeking to minimize transition time the change agent will have to plan carefully the information and exhortation program in light of the degree of participation (in design of the change or in implementation of the change) of those at the various levels of the organization and in view of the degree of trust in management at each level.[22] Where there is no participation, even long-standing trust will waver if the information about the change is so incomplete or ambiguous that an individual faces an unpredictable future. In these circumstances it becomes critically important who (consultant or client spokesman) says what and when. When multiple organization units are being changed in sequence, it is difficult to avoid some resistance to change if the units awaiting their turn for conversion do not have complete and unambiguous information.

In summary, in context of the theoretical development to date, this case pinpoints two major ideas that deserve special attention in future models of planning for organization change. First, there seems to be a drift away from the economic realities of business enterprise. The so-called "conversion" approaches seem to give low priority to time as a scarce and expensive resource. Particularly important is this oversight when the enterprise seeks a specific economic goal. The promise of goal achievement through the mediacy of collaboratively developed social change can be judged as reasonable only after an evaluation of the time interval between change-agent intervention and goal achievement. Such consideration has not been given to time as an economic value. This case shows that time must be a major dimension in any organization change-planning model. Second, the proponents of the "conversion" approaches have so focused on the social system that they have progressed little in an apprecia-

---

22In a small way this research has shown the predictive value of the resistance-to-change model presented by The Foundation for Research on Human Behavior, *op. cit.*, p. 69.

tion of the leverage to be achieved in changing organizational be-havior by technological or structural alterations—what we have called systemic alterations. Little is known about the power of systemic alterations in initiating change, maintaining change in process, or institutionalizing behavioral changes. Yet the consultant's rather effective use of systemic alterations should warn of the incomplete-ness of planning models that include only laboratory training-type intervention strategies and leave no room for intervention strategies based on systemic alterations.

CHAPTER EIGHT

Conclusions—The Control of Change

INTRODUCTION

THROUGHOUT THE CONDUCT of this study, consultant, client executives, and insurance company employees at all levels asked the researcher: "How is the new system working?" The researcher usually phrased the response in terms of how closely a particular regular manager's current behavior, or the behavior of all of a branch's personnel, conformed to the behavior proposed by the consultant. When the researcher himself inquired of these same parties about how the new system was working, he received data on percent of objective achieved, lapse control, expenses per dollar of NPM 1, and the like. Despite a system for controlling the change in transition installed by the consultant, in no one place, at any level, was there the use of *systematic* information bringing together *both* types of data—intermediate, objective, measures of relative conversion and standard performance measures. Attention seemed centered on end results measured in the standard performance indices mentioned above. Yet it would seem that meaningful control would require the combined use of both types of data.

Before pursuing this thought further, it will be instructive to understand some detail of the formal system of control designed by client and consultant and something of its use in practice; then we can begin to build a model for effectively controlling the first-line supervisor's transition from a staff to a line position. (This chapter ends with an inquiry into the more general applicability of the proposed model in controlling any planned change of organization behavior.)

THE CONTROL SYSTEM IN USE BY CLIENT AND CONSULTANT

The new branch marketing plan set up an information-flow system that gave very sophisticated control data on end results. The New Performance Measure, on which the system is based, has been recognized by the industry as an innovation for participating or mutual insurance companies. With each branch—now the equivalent of a profit center, setting annual objectives in NPM and reporting progress against those objectives weekly—control of end results is efficiently set up. Each successively higher level in the hierarchy receives these control data in less detail: branch manager—by agent, regional manager—by regular manager, territory vice president—by branch. Each level can compare actual against planned results in a timely fashion and in appropriate detail to take the necessary supervisory steps.

The consultant also provided for information about behavior. At least, there is provision for each successive level knowing about the subordinate's plans for time allocation. Within the branch the regular manager each week sees the agent's day-by-day plans for prospecting and selling, and he checks at the end of each week on the agent's performance against the plan (an optional system based on Form 06, which is used by about half the regular managers). The regular manager himself writes out and gives the branch manager his time usage plans on a quarterly and a monthly basis. Quarterly, he specifies the number of days to be taken up by fixed demand on his time, the number of days of training planned for each agent, and the subject of the clinical or individual training to be given in each case. Monthly, the regular manager plans time usage day by day, anticipating specifically open agency service time, time for recruiting, training time for specific agents, and subjects for unit conferences, as well as time for his regularly scheduled in-office duties. The branch manager can control regular manager actual time allocation against these quarterly and monthly plans by his day-to-day supervision and especially in his weekly conference with the regular manager. The regular manager himself makes no formal written report of how he adhered to his plans.[1] The branch manager, however, periodically does make a written evaluation of his regular man-

---

[1] About six months after the completion of this study, the company designed a new form for the regular manager's use in *weekly* planning and in recording actual results compared to these plans.

agers (every two months in the first year and semiannually or quarterly thereafter). Ratings (excellent, good, fair, poor) are given each regular manager for his performance in weekly conferences with agents, unit conferences, field work with agents, motivation of agents, organization of time, and recruiting and selection. Then an overall rating is assigned (see Appendix VI for the *Rating Guide* given branch managers). This control process is designed to help the branch manager plan the use of his own time on a priority basis. Also, these periodic ratings are meant to aid the regional manager in diagnosing the needs of a branch during his postconversion visits.

The branch manager plans his own quarter and month in about the same detail as the regular manager. Quarterly, he indicates in order of priority which regular managers need how many days of what specific kind of training. In his 30-day work plan the branch manager specifies day by day with whom he will spend his day and in what activity. The regional manager receives these plans but has no way of being informed about adherence to the plans except during his programmed postconversion follow-up visits (a minimum of three in the first six months) and during the later, less frequent, supervisory visits. The regional manager makes a written evaluation of the branch manager quarterly during the first year and semiannually thereafter. He rates the branch manager overall and on the following points (see Appendix VII for the *Rating Guide*) : short-range goals, long-range goals, developing regular managers, conduct of weekly conferences, organizing time, maintaining branch morale. The regional manager uses these evaluations to determine the priorities in allocating his time. A comparable system is employed between regional manager and territorial vice president, as well as between territorial vice president and senior vice president.

Supplementing this formal control system for behavioral data is the direct feedback to the home office Conversion Coordination Unit from regional managers and even from branch managers. The very nature of this unit's task puts it into daily (phone and written) contact with managers in the field. Though this is not systematic feedback concerning relative conversion of behavior, it is important data for the policy maker.

We might summarize the dual control system in use by client and consultant as in Exhibit 8–1. Note the following points about this dual system for controlling the change in transition:

1. At each level there is automatic and systematic feedback of end results, achieved in the position two levels lower in the organization, measured in objective performance indices that can be compared against plan.
2. Financial rewards at each level are tied to the achievement measured in these performance indices.
3. At each level there is automatic transmittal of planned time usage that indirectly provides the superior with some idea of the defects in the behavior of the man in the position two levels below his own. Only the direct superior has access to feedback

EXHIBIT 8–1

Dual Control System

Performance Indices	Position	Data on Behavior
Performance against plan—by region—access to performance data in full detail monthly	Policy maker	Quarterly and monthly plan of time usage by territorial vice president Feedback on behavior in scheduled monthly conferences and in normal supervision More detailed, though random, feedback from conversion unit
Performance against plan—by branch—monthly	Territorial vice president	Quarterly and monthly plan of time usage by regional manager Feedback on behavior in scheduled monthly conferences
Performance against plan—by unit—weekly and monthly	Regional manager	Quarterly and monthly plan of time usage by branch manager Feedback on behavior in follow-up and supervisory conferences Periodic written evaluation of branch manager
Performance against plan—by agent—weekly and monthly	Branch manager	Quarterly and monthly plan of time usage by regular manager Feedback on behavior in weekly conference and in daily supervision Periodic written evaluation of regular manager
Performance against plan—by agent—weekly and monthly	Regular manager	Weekly plan of time usage by agent Feedback in weekly conference and in daily supervision

on performance against these plans, and only within the branch is there opportunity for continual feedback in the daily supervision.

4. Data on planned behavior are quantifiable in terms of time units (activities and interactions) but are not presented in a systematic format that would allow easy comparison of actual behavior against planned behavior.

5. Ratings for evaluations at each level depend on subjective judgment and inference, not objective recording of observable phenomena.

6. The two types of feedback, performance indices and behavior data, are not reported together in the information-flow system.

7. There is no systematic feedback of behavior data from the regular manager level to the policy level.

This control system can and does work within certain limits. It is predictable that the more quantified performance indices that reflect financial reward prospects would receive first priority attention at all levels. While this is generally so within branches, the skilled branch manager can use the two types of information in diagnosis prior to taking appropriate corrective action. The regional manager has access to sketchy feedback data on branch manager behavior, but if he is perceptive on frequent enough branch visits he can control the change in transition reasonably well. Were it not for the nonsystematic feedback about regular manager behavior from the Conversion Unit, policy makers could not effectively make judgments about the conversion plans or the system itself. By inference in this critique of the control system used by client and consultant we have developed the requirements for a model control system. Of prime importance is the need we have identified for two types of data—performance data and behavior data. This need can be demonstrated with real cogency.

THE NEED FOR A PARTICULAR TYPE OF DUAL FEEDBACK

First, on the level of supervisory control, the branch manager, for instance, needs a system that assures clear identification of the character of deviations through accurate diagnosis. How hazardous it would be to judge a regular manager as unsuccessful because his performance indices have not improved or to judge a regular manager as successful because he behaved as proposed. The branch manager cannot make a diagnosis accurate enough to be the basis for appropriate corrective action unless he recognizes that the regular manager could fit into any one of four situations at any point in time (see Exhibit 8–2).

EXHIBIT 8–2

Four Possible Types of Situations to Be Controlled

	IMPROVED PERFORMANCE	NO IMPROVED PERFORMANCE
CONVERTED	1	2
NOT CONVERTED	3	4

It makes a great deal of difference to the one controlling the regular manager during the transition whether he fits into cell 1, 2, 3, or 4. Different action is called for from the controller. Cell 1 describes the best situation and would call for reinforcement of the regular manager's current behavior. Cell 4 describes a bad, but predictable, situation that calls for a concentrated effort to bring the regular manager's activities, interactions, and sentiments into line with the proposed pattern—a first priority task. Cell 3 describes a potentially dangerous situation that requires about the same attention as the cell 4 case with almost the same priority. Possibly one agent is carrying the unit, or maybe the regular manager himself is doing the bulk of the selling. Success is exacting a penalty somewhere, and a day of reckoning is coming. Cell 2 describes an unpleasant but less dangerous situation. Here the regular manager may need help in getting the agents in line or in replacing nonproductive agents—a lower priority task than called for in the cell 4 and cell 3 cases. If only standard performance measures were examined, serious mistakes could be made in cell 3 (by rewarding the regular manager for short-run improved performance) and cell 2 (by insisting on different behavior from the regular manager already converted but facing peculiar manpower problems on his unit).

Client and consultant would seem to have a need for these same two types of data for a policy level control of the change in transition. Implicit in the installation of such a new system is a dual prediction that is really an hypothesis: (1) the plans for effecting the change in fact will produce the desired behavior patterns, and (2) the proposed behavior patterns will bring about the objective of more economical growth through the positioning of resources with potential in the most promising market niche. Superior competence in the theory of management and vast experience in the application of management principles and techniques (within many industries including insurance) made the consultant very confident of the second part of the prediction—if people behaved as proposed, the company would attain its goals. However, built into the second part of the prediction was the realization that there would be a lag between converted behavior and improvement in results (Exhibit 8–3).

EXHIBIT 8–3
Time Lag between Conversion and Improvement

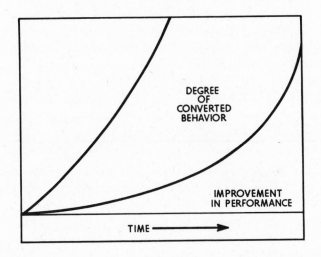

Watching only measures of end results, then, becomes inappropriate control during transition. In addition, the consultant is understandably less confident of the first part of the prediction—that his plans will effect conversion. This consulting firm, probably more than any major management consulting firm, is sensitive to the complexities involved in changing organizational behavior. Every effort is made by this firm to learn more about organizational change in internal lectures and discussions and external seminars with social scientists working in this area. The firm showed its serious interest by not only allowing but encouraging this unprecedented study. All this interest and effort notwithstanding, the hypothesis about the effectiveness of its plans for producing change had to be verified. This could not be done without some intermediary measure of behavior patterns in transition. It would matter a great deal at the policy level to both client and consultant whether the trend in this combined data feedback indicated the change process was producing situation 1, 2, 3, or 4 (see Exhibit 8–2) . Recall that not all branches were to be converted at once, so lessons learned in earlier conversions could modify the conversion plans and even the system itself for later conversions. If feedback on behavior patterns and end results showed a tendency for situation 1 (converted behavior and improved results) to exist, policy makers would feel encouraged to go ahead with the conversion's plans, as is, with firmer confidence in the dual prediction. If there seemed to be a tendency toward situation 2 (converted behavior but no marked improvement in results) , policy makers would again find confirmation of the first part of the prediction and hence would continue on with the conversion process. However, a judgment would have to be made as regards the second part of the prediction. Is the expected transitional lag between converted behavior and end result improvement too long? Attention would be directed to the questions: Is our agent manpower qualified to do the job? Have we given the converted branch personnel the best competitive marketing tools in terms of product portfolio, promotion support, and price as attractive as competent underwriting will permit? Or more radically, are the behavior patterns proposed suitable for the task—a challenge to the second part of the prediction? If situation 3 (unconverted behavior but improved results) seems to exist and persist, policy makers face the decision whether to revise the conversion plans on the assumption that the improved results are artificial and cannot be maintained without converted behavior or to go ahead as planned on the assumption that the improvements are a "Hawthorne effect." That is, maybe the branch personnel just needed a challenge, some attention from top management, to needle them into better production. Policy makers facing persistent situation 4 (unconverted behavior and no improved results) would certainly want to reexamine the conversion plans before going ahead with the new system in other branches.

To control the change process in transition, whether as day-to-day supervisor or as policy maker, requires continual access to systematic information of two kinds: intermediate, objective, measures of relative conversion and standard performance indices. The control system employed by client and consultant went part of the way toward meeting the need for this particular type of dual feedback. An ideal or model system would demand a somewhat tighter definition of behavior data, a more formalized data gathering and transmission system, and a continuous evaluation of the synthesized product of the "control system" (for statistical performance data) and the "monitor system" (for behavior data).

A MODEL SYSTEM FOR CONTROLLING THE CHANGE IN TRANSITION

In the spirit of the new system that emphasizes responsible, personal supervision by line management, the system for controlling the change in transition should operate through the newly structured chain of command. The controls may well be temporary. Controls for on-the-line supervision may be phased out as behavior at each level approaches the proposed patterns and marked improvement appears in performance indices. The evaluation system for policy level control may be discontinued when the dual hypothesis has been verified: (1) the plans for effecting the change will in fact produce the desired behavior patterns, and (2) the proposed behavior patterns will bring about more economical growth.

The "control system" that already exists for standard performance indices will serve admirably as one leg of a model system. This would be joined, however, to a "monitor system" providing more systematic data about behavior so that supervisor and policy maker can watch the joint trend and make appropriate control decisions. The two types of data should probably be reported together so that attention will not be exclusively captured by the performance indices because of their relationship to financial rewards. Both supervisor and policy maker would be required to synthesize the twofold feedback at each point during the transition so that a trend could be plotted in a progress chart (Exhibit 8–4) that corresponds to Exhibit 8–2. The curve on the chart approximates the path expected by the consultants, indicating the lag between relative behavior conversion and relative improvement in performance indices (see Exhibit 8–3).

To permit individual supervisors as well as policy makers to use trends in progress charts as the basis for control, ideally there should be (1) a standard of behavior; (2) a way of objectively observing and reporting; and (3) access to systematic feedback about actual behavior for comparison against standard. This means that in each

EXHIBIT 8–4
Progress Chart Showing Predicted Path of Regular Manager
Behavioral and Performance Change

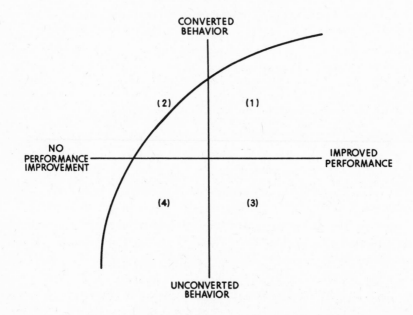

supervisory relationship the superior would have to observe the subordinate's behavior directly or receive data in the information-flow system that would be verifiable evidence of behavior. Because of the dependence of subordinate on superior in the change process, superior A may get corroborative evidence of subordinate B's behavior from data about sub-subordinate C's behavior. That is, a superior who cannot collect his own feedback by personal observation will probably have to receive data about both his subordinate and his subordinate's subordinate—each supervisory control unit would extend over three levels of the organization. It should be noted, however, that behavioral data about regional managers (two levels below the policy makers) will not serve the policy makers in their control function. The only way policy makers can verify the twofold hypothesis implicit in the planned change is by checking the progress chart trends of the regular manager position. Conversion at the regular manager level and performance improvement of the regular manager's unit tell the story as nothing else will. Consequently, the policy makers need timely access to progress charts of regular managers, not for supervisory control (which would do violence to the system) , but for policy control of the plans for effecting the change and of the proposed system itself. Under these circumstances, the regional manager might deviate from the line channels of upward communications and funnel the progress charts directly to the Conversion Coordination Unit in the home office. This unit, then, could appraise policy makers of evolving trends in the progress charts of regular managers' converted two quarters, four quarters, and so forth.

Such a model for supervisory and policy control is not without difficulties. Expressing standard behavior in terms of observable phenomena raises a philosophical and a threefold operational issue. The use of "quantified" standards of behavior for control purposes smacks of procedural control, part of the managerial philosophy the consultant very much wanted to replace with end result control. However, if there is to be meaningful control of the process of change, some control must be exercised over behavior. Such control necessitates intermediary measures of relative conversion. During the transition, behavior itself has to be viewed as an end, not just as a means to achieve the end of better performance indices. Operationally, first there is the question of the possibility of capsuling a manager's function in a "quantified" standard. Traditionally, the manager's function has been expressed in terms of leading subordinates, motivating subordinates, and the like. Comparing actual behavior against a standard expressed in such terms becomes at best a difficult inferential process. Recent attempts by "interactionists," using concepts from applied anthropology to view the managerial function in terms of observable phenomena, have provided a somewhat more workable approach. The researcher chose to view the manager's job in this study in interactionist terms—activities, interactions, and sentiments —and is convinced that such a portrayal can validly depict a manager's function. Even so, two further problems remain. A superior who has continual and direct contact with his subordinate may be able to collect behavioral data by observation. But how can a superior who has several subordinate managers from whom he may be geographically distant most of the time observe behavior? Such is the case in the regional manager–branch manager relationship. Provided there is some opportunity to observe his subordinate and his subordinate's subordinates at least periodically, a superior may observe behavior by monitoring structured diaries of the men in the positions in the next two lower levels. Such a monitoring process may begin by a check of the immediate subordinate's time usage plan for the next week or month to see that it reflects an attempt to conform to standard behavior. Then the subordinate keeps a diary of actual time usage. The subordinate repeats this same process— plan and diary—with his subordinates. The superior compares his subordinate's diary, corroborated by his sub-subordinates' diaries, with the approved time usage plan. This done, the superior is finally ready to combine the degree of converted behavior with the performance indices in order to plot his subordinate's current position on the progress chart. Such an evaluation system is not set forth as a proposal, but as an example indicative of the requirements for effective behavioral control where the superior (the regional manager, for instance) cannot directly observe his subordinate's (the branch manager's) behavior. Direct observation could replace the diaries in the branch manager–regular manager relationship.

The final operational issue in behavior control arises from the theoretical difficulties with any index. If "nonconverted" to "converted" is a continuum along which current behavior is to be plotted, activities-interactions-sentiments must be converted into an index number. Each element of behavior itself could be plotted along a continuum: "nonconverted" to "converted." The index of relative behavior conversion could be represented as follows: $RBC = (f) \Delta A + \Delta I + \Delta S$, relative behavior conversion is a function of the degree of change in activities plus the degree of change in interactions plus the degree of change in sentiments. Such an expression assumes the elements are additive and equally weighted. This knotty issue is raised here not because the researcher has a creative solution, but as a frank admission that the interactionist approach (using quantifiable categories to describe behavior) has to cope with the same difficulties as the consultant's more qualitative approach. The consultant proposed an evaluation of the regular manager, for instance, that involved the assignment of an overall rating of excellent, good, fair, or poor on the basis of six like ratings in individual areas of management skill. The consultant did design a creative index of performance measures in NPM 2, but a univalued index of relative behavior conversion for interactionist or consultant still requires an artful management judgment.

IMPLICATIONS FOR THE THEORY OF CONTROL IN ORGANIZATION CHANGE PROGRAMS

As pointed out in Chapter One, the literature contains some recent studies aimed at evaluating organization change programs. Often these evaluative efforts view change as an event and not as a process; hence, the approaches mean little to an operating manager who must keep a change program "on track" during the transition from "before" to "after." Analysis of this case suggests that no effort to control the process of changing organization behavior will be fully successful unless consideration is given the following four points:[2]

First, behavior data *and* economic performance data must be used in the control effort. Otherwise, dangerous diagnostic errors could be made at both the supervisory and policy-maker levels. Change program effectiveness is not gauged by measures of behavior change *or* measures of performance improvement. Change program effectiveness can be gauged only by the composite or synthesized index made up of both the behavior and performance measures.

Second, since measurable performance change so often lags behavioral change, the controller must use some such diagnostic device as the four-cell matrix in Exhibit 8-2 or the two-dimensional progress chart in Exhibit 8-4 in order to properly identify the existing situation. Only such a device prevents the common naive attempt to judge a change program in the unidimensional world of "success" and place it somewhere on a successful-unsuccessful continuum. Only such a device permits the controller to verify the twofold hypothesis implicit in any planned change program.

Third, while present "control systems" probably provide adequate data on economic performance, a parallel "monitor system" for data on relative behavior change is often lacking. Even if the "monitor system" did exist, the fact that all rewards and sanctions are tied to the performance indices reflected in the "control system" means that the latter often receives unbalanced attention at supervisory if not at policy-maker control levels. It may be transitionally necessary to consider distributing rewards and sanctions on the basis of the synthesized index of both the "control" and the "monitor" systems' data.

---

[2]See Appendix V for a technical note about the character of the conclusions derived from a case study such as this.

Fourth, behavior data must be of a character to express comprehensively and validly the behavior proposed by the change agent as well as actual postconversion behavior. Attitude data do not always tell the whole story, nor do they always give a valid picture. Ideally, some objective and verifiable behavior data are needed as the raw material for the "monitor system." The observational approach used in this case study (activities, interactions, and sentiments) could not be called optimal. As pointed out in the last section, the observational approach could very easily bear the stigma of procedural control (though, possibly, sophisticated sampling techniques could make it a less burdensome data-gathering method). Also, the observational approach used here seems to offend the law of parsimony because of built-in duplications. It should be noted, too, that the three-dimensional model of behavior is a particularly blunt instrument for capturing the richness and nuances of human behavior. Finally, the difficulty of reducing the three dimensions to one index value for plotting on the progress chart (see Exhibit 8–4) stands in the way of the observational approach's being immediately operational. Possibly, multiple plottings of separate activity, interaction, and sentiment measures may lead to the empirical determination of one of them as a reliable indicator of relative behavioral change.

In summary, neither client nor consultant can give a fully satisfactory answer to "How is the new system working?" unless he synthesizes valid behavior data, systematically fed back in a "monitor system," with performance data from the "control system" on a chart showing the two-dimensional progress of the planned change effort.

CHAPTER NINE

The Manager and Organizational Innovation

In discussions with operating managers concerning this story of the consultant as change agent some interesting perspectives have appeared. These final pages will reflect those discussions and switch the spotlight from consultant to manager. This chapter departs from the pattern of the previous ones which described and explained the change effort. Here the emphasis is on reaction to the consultant's part in the reorganization of the insurance company—reaction from the viewpoint of operating managers.

CREATIVITY AND INNOVATION

Just as every consultant doubtless has a bottom drawer somewhere full of thick reports that are monuments to scorned advice, nearly every manager must have a cobwebbed file of creative ideas on what should be done in his organization. In a very deflating article Theodore Levitt fingered the sore spot when he said, "Creativity Is Not Enough!"[1] Creativity is the conception of an idea; innovation is the birth of change. The analogy is apt in more than one respect. In the economy of the manager's function, the payoff comes only to change. While the manager may find it temporarily exciting to work in an environment charged with creative ideas, true satisfaction comes only when the manager bridges the creativity-innovation gap. Knowing *what* to do is less important than knowing *how to do it*.

In the reorganization of the insurance company, as previously dis-

---

[1]Levitt, Theodore, "Creativity Is Not Enough," *Harvard Business Review*, Vol. 41, No. 3, May-June, 1963.

cussed, the consultant is not threatened by the allegation put forth by some insurance company executives that he proposed scarcely anything new. The consultant produced organizational innovation. From the viewpoint of the operating manager, the consultant's expertise in implementing creative change programs may be his most valued and envied quality. It would be misleading to imply that implementation is a discrete step in a sequential process moving from problem identification to follow-up. Implementation is a phase of a more complex process in which implementation-oriented activity takes place right along with the early phases of problem identification, diagnosis, etc. In this light, the operating manager's temptation to hire the consultant to install an already-designed organizational change makes little sense. Management is finding it increasingly difficult to find consultants to wear the implementer's hat because so often it turned out to be the executioner's hood. In fact, most good consultants will attempt to do their own study of organizational needs partly as recognition of the fact that what goes on in these early phases of the change program affects the chances of successfully bridging the creativity-innovation gap.

One other management tendency in the use of consultants deserves challenge on the grounds it ignores the place of implementation in the change process. By "guess-timation," over two thirds of the billion dollars annually spent on consultants in this country pay for data gathering or diagnostic studies which terminate with the huge report of findings, conclusions, and recommendations. The consultant is not allowed to—or maybe more importantly, is not required to—demonstrate his expertise in producing innovation. Many managers (and consultants too!) at times seem unaware that implementation has already started when the consultant moves from department to department or plant to plant collecting data. A strong case can be made for involving the consultant as change agent throughout the entire change process. With this approach the consultant must view the process as a whole and his behavior as part of a coherent strategy for producing innovation. The operating manager need not lose control of his organization during the consultant's involvement. As a matter of fact, the requirement that the consultant be involved in the whole change process probably insures that the consultant will cultivate and utilize the operating manager throughout the change process. This burdens the consultant to expand his repertoire of behaviors so that he can be truly responsive to the client's need. If this practice became common in the consulting industry, those consultants still selling a product (a pre-packaged panacea solution for some organizational need) would lose out to those offering a genuine service. The service is the bridging of the creativity-innovation gap by a change agent.

Isn't it an admission of management ineptness to require an outsider as change agent? This issue nags the operating manager. Greiner[2] found that the appearance of an individual new to the organization was associated with the more successful change efforts reported in the literature. The new individual is not always a consultant. He may appear in the normal course of managerial succession. In Greiner's analysis this new individual was influential in the power redistribution which characterized the successful change programs. In the reorganization of the insurance company the consultant's presence and behavior reinforced a power redistribution already underway in the normal course of managerial succession. Many of those involved on both sides of the consultant-client relationship felt that while change was in the wind, the reorganization would not have been so boldly nor so quickly accomplished without the consultant's involvement. This assertion does not indict the management for incompetence or intransigence. To find explanation solely in the shifting of power and the dynamics of bargaining coalitions where the consultant swings the weight toward innovation seems too simplistic. The organization is something more than a purely political system. How can we explain that a consultant may innovate where a manager alone stews in creative frustration? Can the organization be as irrational as some managers insist when they offer as the cause: "No prophet is honored in his own country"? Maybe so many managers are frustrated as change agents because there is a form of schizophrenia built into their managerial function.

MAINTENANCE AND INNOVATION

The operating manager has a twofold function. He must maintain the system; that is, keep up the flow of goods and services at a profit. He must also innovate within the system itself in terms of what the system does and how the system performs. In maintaining the system the manager expects certain characteristics to predominate. Main-

---

[2]Greiner, Larry E., "Patterns of Organization Change," *Harvard Business Review*, Vol. 45, No. 3, May-June 1967.

tenance calls for more predictability than uncertainty, more stability than dynamism, more control than freedom, more conformity than divergence, more programmed behavior than unprogrammed behavior. In the long view maintenance also requires innovation lest obsolescence, sclerosis, or the pathology labeled "organizational dry rot" by John Gardner[3] set in. The manager, then, finds himself fostering system characteristics like uncertainty, dynamism, freedom, divergence, and unprogrammedness. The sensible manager, however, knows that innovation cannot flourish in unconstrained, anarchic activity so he attempts to move back along the continuum from freedom toward control, for instance. In simple terms, you cannot maintain a system without innovation nor can you innovate without maintaining the system. The manager faces the challenge of balancing the maintenance demands and the innovation demands. Continually there are conflicts to be managed and tradeoffs to be measured. Driven on by a host of proselytizing academicians—the manager forges ahead on the holy-grail search for the optimum point along a half a dozen control-freedom type continua.

In the excitement of this managerial balancing act (which is really only indicative of a multidimensional world of conflict management) the maintenance aspect of the manager's function seems to get more attention. Why not, since we have a complex of measures which satisfies the manager's and his superiors' pressing need for virtually "real-time" evaluative feedback? What has happened in some organizations is that the operating manager is specialized as the maintenance man (and some resent the derogatory connotation to the label!). Innovation is left to the staff specialist (internal consultant) or outside consultant. While the operating manager may yen for the change agent role, the maintenance aspect of his function consumes his time, narrows his vision, truncates his time horizon, saps his energy, and in sum seduces his attention to the flow of goods and services through the system. What is more, the operating manager, by this emphasis on maintenance, may condition his colleagues to expect bureaucratic sorts of behavior from him and to reciprocate with behavior that smacks of the bureaucratic. With valid reason, then, the operating manager may call in a consultant to break the cycle, so to speak, and innovate. By knowing when to seek such help and how to use the consultant, the manager may accomplish his inno-

---

[3]Gardner, John W., "How to Prevent Organizational Dry Rot," *Harpers,* October 1965.

vative function as he may in no other way. This seems to be especially so when the organizational innovation is tantamount to a 180-degree turn as it was in the insurance company described in this research. Without denying that the consultant gains efficacy as a change agent from his special analytic and synthesis skills, from his objectivity, and so forth, our point here is that the consultant has the edge because he is not involved in nor associated with the past or present maintenance of the system.

WHAT KIND OF CONSULTATION TO EMPLOY

We have already argued in Chapter Seven that, once a manager decides to seek a consultant's help, his problematic situation dictates the appropriate kind of consultation. The entry conditions in his system guide the preference for the more unilateral or collaborative change agent role, for the consultant who focuses more on the social or on the technical aspect of the system, and for the change agent whose intervention strategies tend more to produce compliance or conversion. The behavior of the consultant in the reorganization of the insurance company seems to fit the expectations of most managers who have discussed this research. However, the more collaborative consultant who seeks to change organizations especially through conversion of the social system is becoming better known in the business community. The question has been raised as to what sorts of differences would there have been for the top operating managers had the consultant behaved more like the latter one described above. The question is only answerable in general terms since we must imagine a kind of modal change agent behavior from the side of a continuum opposite the behavior actually employed by the consultant in the insurance company reorganization.

Had the change process been based on the application of something like Robert Blake's Managerial Grid technique, management would probably have noticed significant differences. Management would have been involved in an effort to reexamine and probably alter the culture of the company, beginning from the top. The individual men at the top would be challenged for a personal commitment to change and develop more interpersonal competence. Each would be involved in introspection on an individual and group level that would seek to uncover and evaluate the consequences of various kinds of behavior. There would have to be tolerance and energy for an open-ended inquiry into dimensions of organizational behavior, dimensions which, in many cases, were probably not previously explored. Such a process predictably would affect the relationships among people at the top and between organizational levels. In all likelihood an increased openness and spirit of inquiry would characterize the personal commitment of the men at the top and subsequently serve as the exemplar for conversion at successively lower levels of the hierarchy. As the social system developed in the new culture, the organization's task performance would come under scrutiny by individuals and groups. The more effective social system would better cope with the demands of the task and would more resourcefully adjust the technical system (formal organization, control system, reward system, information system, etc.) to meet organizational objectives. Crucial to this sort of change process under circumstances like those in the insurance company is that the changes do not cease with the conversion of the social system. A revitalized social system may lead to a worse state if the technical system retains flaws—"new wine in old wine skins. . . ."

As someone has pointed out concerning participative management, the unfreezing and conversion processes set loose energy for change that may lay outside management's original intention, making the management of the changes a real challenge. Management may face not only a longer than anticipated list of changes but also a prolonged period of change in which everything is tentative and undergoing reality testing. It may be difficult to bring cloture to the change process by refreezing or institutionalizing the changes so that the maintenance function in the organization may be efficiently carried out.

If I understand my colleagues correctly, such is a broad brush picture of how managers, especially those at the top, might have been affected had a different sort of change agent been involved. Speculation concerning the relative success of the actual and hypothetical change processes would be vain. Any such comparison, if it were possible, would depend on the choice of evaluation criteria and the time frame employed. The collaborative conversion of the social system would probably take more time and, in the view of some of the practitioners, have deeper and more long-term effects, some of which would not be measurable with our conventional economic measures. Central to the long-term effects would be management's increased capacity to cope with the task of running the insurance company. While managers would have to heavily invest by personal immersion in such a change process, there would be personal and interpersonal dividends. Also important in the promised long-term effects would be the movement of attitudes toward more commitment, more mutual respect, and more trust. It is this new organizational culture which makes for permanance in behavioral changes, in the modified roles played by organizational members. People behave differently because their attitudes have changed and their values have been reexamined. Recall that in the insurance company reorganization the manager's environment was so "engineered" that he had to behave differently. The manager behaved differently because he almost had to in the newly structured environment, not because his attitudes had changed. Edgar Schein warns that such changes might be quite temporary.

In those cases where the direction of the change is itself coerced (as contrasted with letting it occur through identification or internalization), it is highly unlikely that anything is accomplished other than surface behavioral change in the target. And such surface change will be abandoned the moment the coercive force of the change agent is lessened.[4]

In the insurance company case, of course, the "coercive force" is the newly designed system (authority, reward, information, work flow, physical) and not some ephemeral threat. The behavioral changes may well stick and the relevant attitudes may develop through a process somewhat like the one described by Schein.

If the behavioral changes are coerced at the same time as other unfreezing operations are undertaken, actual influence can be facilitated if the individual find himself having to learn attitudes to justify the kinds of behavior he has been forced to exhibit. The salesman may not have an attitude of cynicism toward his customers initially. If, however, he is forced by his boss to behave as if he felt cynical, he might develop real cynicism as a way of justifying his actual behavior.[5]

The consultant in the insurance company reorganization did not leave the culture untouched. The culture changed—but by a process somewhat more indirect than would be employed by a collaborative change agent in his conversion of the social system. For the collaborative change agent the organizational innovation may be viewed as

---

    [4]Schein, Edgar H., "Management Development as a Process of Influence," *Industrial Management Review*, II, No. 2 (May, 1961).
    [5]*Ibid.*

the product of a particular type of cultural change from the top of the organization on down. The "peritus" change agent in the insurance company reorganization proposed an organizational innovation which impacted with the existing culture, causing it to shift into a form that is still evolving.

This last point brings us face to face with the issue that so many wish to ignore. Change agents have values. Not all have the same values. Consciously or unconsciously these normative postures affect the behavior of the change agent. The operating manager would be well advised to check his own criteria for successful organizational innovation against his prospective change agent's vision of what an organization should be. So often managers pose the issue as: "Which can do more harm, an incompetent 'head shrinker' or an amateur at organizational scrabble?" A more profitable inquiry is: "Who can do more good in this organization at this time, a change agent who collaboratively converts the social system or a change agent who more or less unilaterally focuses on the technical system and produces behavioral change through an 'engineering' of the structural environment?" The answer depends on the manager's definition of "good" as well as on the conditions facing the consultant when he enters the client system.

Draft of a Letter to Managers of Branches
To Be Visited by the Consulting Firm

As YOU KNOW, we are continually engaged in a program of evaluating our operations to determine what opportunities for improvement exist.

In line with this continuing program, we have asked a management consulting firm with considerable experience in the life insurance business as well as other industries to make an especially broad study covering all aspects of our personal life insurance sales operations.

As part of this study, representatives of this firm will be visiting a number of our branch offices during the next month. We have selected your office among others in a sample intended to give our consultants exposure to the various kinds of markets in which we operate.

During the visit—which will probably require about two days—the consultant will, of course, want to talk extensively with you about the nature of your operations. In addition, we would like you to arrange for him to spend some time with at least two of your assistant managers and two of your agents, as well as any other personnel you and he may decide would be helpful in providing the kind of information they need. The particular member of the consulting firm who will be visiting your office will call you sometime during the next few weeks to arrange a mutually convenient date and to discuss with you the kind of interviewing schedule he would like you to arrange.

Please feel free to make available to the consultant any information he requests and to be perfectly candid in your conversations with him. I know that you will do your utmost to cooperate in this important project.

Outline of Consultant's Findings
And Recommendations[1]
(Oral Report Given in Late 1961 and Early 1962)

PREPARING SALES MANAGEMENT FOR THE CHALLENGES
AND OPPORTUNITIES AHEAD

I.—*The Changing Market Environment for Life Insurance*
   A. Market Trends
      1. The market opportunity is changing substantially in terms of the basic characteristics of the potential insurance buyer.
      2. The market opportunity is also changing in terms of its geographic location.
      3. The overall rate of change is accelerating.
   B. Industry Developments
      1. Industry trends and developments reflect these changes in market opportunity.
      2. The industry moved with the market as the major potential for premium payments shifted into higher family income levels.

---

[1]This outline presents in briefest form—largely in the consultant's words—the content of a 110-page document with 87 exhibits that itself was merely the basis for an oral presentation. (The remarks in parentheses are the researcher's.) It should be read only for an appreciation of the dimensions of the consulting assignment. The richness, cogency, and balance of the original are lost in this outline because the detail, design, and production of the document cannot be reproduced here.

3. Higher income families became recognized as best individual prospects.
4. Life insurance companies faced increased competition.
5. Costs of doing business rose sharply throughout the industry.

C. Impact of Environmental Changes on Sales Representative's Job
1. Role of the combination (selling and collecting) agent is different today from what it has been in the past.
2. Sales opportunities are changing.
3. Because the market environment has not changed uniformly throughout the country, the sales representative and sales management jobs today vary significantly from area to area and even from branch to branch within the same area.

II.—*The Company's Adaptation to These Environmental Changes*
A. Adaptive Moves the Company Has Made
1. The special agent program was launched and built up rapidly in 1957, 1958, and 1959.
2. Concerted efforts are being made to expand in areas where growth has lagged.
3. Manpower reductions are being made in some branches, while expansion is being pushed more selectively than it was in 1958 and 1959.
4. The company's policy portfolio has been modernized.
5. Compensation plans for agents, Branch Managers, and Assistant Managers have been revised to make them more sensitive to production results and to reduce the distinction between account (where premiums are collected weekly or monthly) and notice (premiums are mailed in) business.
6. Increased attention has been given to sales promotion.
7. The Regional Manager plan has been launched on a pilot-installation basis.

B. Results Achieved by the Company in Adapting to Environmental Changes
1. These moves have enabled the company, within the past five years, to achieve overall end results in sales and service that compare favorably with industry results.
2. But, despite generally satisfactory current results, trends

and developments within individual elements of performance raise questions as to how adequately and economically the company is adapting, for the long pull, to many important environmental changes that are taking place.

III.—*A Recommended Program for Meeting Future Requirements*
Introduction: As we understand it, the company is dedicated to serving the best interests of its policyholders, its employees, and the public by achieving the following objectives:

1. To provide each policyholder with prompt, courteous, and efficient service.
2. To prevent lapses that can be avoided at reasonable cost.
3. To write an increasing amount of new business.
4. To maintain investment yields and operating expenses at optimum levels.

We believe that Sales Management's contribution to these objectives is best reflected in one overall measure of performance. (Since a mutual insurance company does not use profit as a performance measure, a measure had to be designed which took account of net sales dollars—net premiums—and costs. The consultants here proposed such a new measure, which we will call New Performance Measure—N.P.M.)

The basic and never-ending managerial task confronting Sales Management—as with any large-scale organization—is the development of timely and effective responses to shifts in the environmental forces at work. And although, as we have pointed out, the company has already made some sound changes in its continuing effort to adjust to the environment, we believe that two additional programs of change are needed.

Part One—Gearing the Company's Market Strategy to the Major Market Opportunities of the Future

A. Increasing the Company's Penetration of the Most Attractive Income Segments of the Market
B. Achieving Optimum Manpower Growth and Development in the Most Attractive Markets

(Note: Under both of these headings detailed marketing strategy was proposed—a specific guide to resource allocation policy by market segment—which obviously cannot be reproduced here.)

Part Two—Strengthening the Management of Sales Representative Activities

Introduction:
1. Effective implementation of the market strategy just outlined and the changes it requires is essential if the company is to be properly "positioned"—both geographically and by income level segment—to capitalize on the major market opportunities of the future.
2. By themselves, however, these changes do not represent a total response to the environmental forces at work. This second part of our recommendations discusses the additional programs of change needed—strengthening the management of branch activities. In summary, this four part program is aimed at developing a dynamic frontline sales management capable of significantly increasing the productivity of the individual agent without an offsetting increase in expenses.
3. Importance of strong branch management. Strong branch management has traditionally been important, but the more demanding selling environment now emerging is further enlarging the responsibility of branch managers.
A. Developing a More Dynamic Approach to Planning and Controlling Branch Office Operations (Note: Since the recommendations of this section are covered in the body of the study, only a capsule of what the consultants proposed under each heading will appear here. The paraphrase continues through III D.)
1. Increase the proficiency of more Branch Managers in determining market potential, evaluating branch resources, setting meaningful fact-based goals that will produce the optimum end results for the company, spelling out concrete action programs to achieve these programs.
2. Institution of an annual branch operating plan—using the New Performance Measure.
3. Refine the proposed plan in a three- or four-branch pilot test.
4. Train the Regional Managers thoroughly in using the branch operating plan as a basis for working with Branch Managers and for evaluating their performance.
5. Develop a program for training Branch Managers and Assistant Managers in using this approach and managing the operation of their districts.

     6. Train all other levels of sales management in the use of the objective-setting approach as the basis for planning and controlling field activities.

B. Improving the Training and Direction of Branch Managers

     1. The new planning approach for branch operations will strengthen the training and direction of Branch Managers.

     2. Extend the Regional Manager concept nationally.

     3. Develop specific guidelines to assist Regional Managers and Branch Managers in day-to-day execution of their jobs.

     4. Incorporate these guidelines plus the new approach to planning branch operations into the management training program for Branch Managers.

C. Strengthen Compensation and Recognition Plans for Branch Managers

     1. Use the New Performance Measure as the basis for compensation and recognition.

     2. Increase rewards for good performance and penalties for poor performance.

     3. Reduce the average proportion of fixed compensation from 60 to 40 percent.

     4. Standardize the fixed base for all Branch Managers.

     5. Base the variable portion of income on a percentage of branch business measured by N.P.M.

     6. Institute an annual branch objective bonus related to the size of branch objective and percentage of objective achieved.

     7. Protect against unforeseen catastrophes with a "disaster minimum."

     8. Provide a special "development subsidy" where a major building job is needed.

     9. Pay promotion awards—a one-time payment for promotions out of the branch to compensate for the short-term loss in branch results.

    10. Pilot test the new compensation arrangements.

    11. Use percentage of objective achieved (in N.P.M.) as basis for Sales Trophy standing.

D. Increasing the Effectiveness of Assistant Managers

     1. Give Assistant Managers clear-cut responsibility for re-

sults produced (both production and conservation) by men assigned to them full-time.

2. Assign special agent responsibility to supervisors who have the ability to recruit and develop special agents, and require that they devote full time to this job.

3. Adopt a policy of greater flexibility in determining the number and kind of Assistant Managers needed in a particular district.

4. Build the career attractiveness of the Assistant Manager position by (a) changing the title to Regular Manager—Regular Manager for regular agents and Special Manager for special agents[2] and (b) adopting compensation plans for both positions which would have the following elements:

   —a fixed base slightly lower than current average fixed payments, with a 15–20 percent differential for Special Managers.

   —a unit incentive as a percentage of business—measured in N.P.M.—generated by the agents assigned to him.

   —a branch incentive as a percentage of business—measured in N.P.M.—generated by the whole branch put into a pool to be equally divided among all Regular and Special Managers.

   —promotion allowances, disaster minimum, and development subsidy as described above for the Branch Manager.

IV.—*An Approach to Implementing Recommended Changes*

   A. A General Approach to Effecting Change in Large Organizations

   1. The ability of large organizations to make major changes successfully depends on the methods used to effect change and the leadership from top management in bringing about change.

   2. The methods used for effecting major changes successfully vary with the type of change desired. These methods include:

      (a) Preparing detailed plans for a change for which the framework has been developed and agreed on in

---

[2]The force of the title change is lost in the disguised titles used in this study.

principle. Frequently a task force is assigned this responsibility.

(b) Testing complex changes experimentally in selected areas.

(c) Proceeding with implementation in a planned series of digestible steps over a period of time.

3. In addition, major changes inevitably require direct participation of top management.

B. Applying This Approach to the Changes Recommended

1. (A list of recommendations to be translated into detailed plans for change—dealing with special agents, training programs to prepare regular and special agents for the new market strategies, training for the Branch Manager.)

2. We suggest that the implementation of these recommendations be the responsibility primarily of the appropriate home office executives.

3. The following recommendations should be pilot tested in selected branches before being formally introduced:

(a) an approach to planning and controlling branch operations.

(b) restructured branch organization and revised compensation plans for Assistant Managers that pinpoint supervisory responsibility and rewards for each Assistant Manager.

(c) new compensation plan and Sales Trophy basis for Branch Managers.

4. Carrying out these pilot tests will require extensive participation by the consultants and appropriate home office and field personnel.

5. The following recommendations should be carried out over a period of time.

(A list of points, basically marketing strategy)

APPENDIX III

Timetable of Events in the
Consultant-Client Relationship

	JULY	AUGUST	SEPTEMBER	OCTOBER	NOVEMBER	DECEMBER
1960	Internal Branch Management Compensation Committee Formed by Company				Exploratory Talks Begun with Consultants	

	JANUARY	FEBRUARY	MARCH	APRIL	MAY	JUNE
1961			Consulting Proposal Submitted			Consulting Firm Formally Engaged

1962

JULY	AUGUST	SEPTEMBER	OCTOBER	NOVEMBER	DECEMBER
Diagnostic Phase Interviews Analysis Visits to Sample Branches		Research in Progress Feedback work sessions with Senior V.P. and Staff V.P.s		Presentation of Oral Report to Top Management	

JANUARY	FEBRUARY	MARCH	APRIL	MAY	JUNE
Presentation of Oral Report Continues	Approval for Phase II	Program Formulation from General Recommendations		Pilot Test in First 3 Branches	

JULY	AUGUST	SEPTEMBER	OCTOBER	NOVEMBER	DECEMBER
Decision to Expand Pilot Test			6 Branches Added to Pilot Test		

1963

JANUARY	FEBRUARY	MARCH	APRIL	MAY	JUNE
		Branch Managers' Convention	Beginning of National Implementation		

Percent Change by Agency in NPM 1 Year before versus Year after Conversion

Unit of Regular Mgr.:	1A	1C	2A	2C	3B
Percent Change by Unit:	(20%)[1]	14%[2]	(23%)	(44%)[3]	(16.5%)
Percent Change by Agency:	19%	47%	51%	(75%)	(19%)
	(85%)	(54%)	(58%)	(9%)	(35%)
	23%	5%	(29%)	(61%)	(128%)
	(95%)	58%	(75%)	(12%)	26%
	7%	530%	(25%)	(95%)	1700%
	(220%)	(47%)	(38%)	3%	(28%)
	20%	(4%)	95%		19%
					75%

Unit of Regular Mgr.:	3C	3D	5B	5C	5D	6B
Percent Change by Unit:	80%	(106%)	(29%)	(5.5%)	(34%)[4]	(27%)
Percent Change by Agency:	240%	(16%)	55%	(65%)	5%	36%
	43%	(55%)	(34%)	(21%)	(200%)	5%
	460%	(78%)	(81%)	9%	16%	(51%)
	78%	(36%)	(64%)	(18%)	(50%)	31%
	49%	(80%)	5.5%	(45%)	(11%)	(70%)
	< 1%	(26%)	8.2%	68%	(83%)	3%
	(28%)	(9%)				(74%)
	65%					(41%)

Unit of Regular Mgr.:	7A	7B	8A	8B
Percent Change by Unit:	10.3%[5]	(6.4%)[5]	(44.0%)[1]	(7.5%)[1]
Percent Change by Agency:	(6%)	(11%)	58%	(56%)
	19%	24%	(90%)	15%
	(9%)	(1%)	(33%)	200%
	30%	(1%)	(53%)	28%
	71%	(1%)	(77%)	(31%)
	(26%)	17%	(40%)	14%
	49%	6404%	(44%)	(245%)
	(20%)	(26%)		
	25%	(185%)		

( )decrease
[1] Data unavailable for two of the nine agencies.
[2] New agency added after conversion produced double the company average in NPM 1.
[3] Data unavailable for two of the eight agencies.
[4] New agency added after conversion produced about the company average in NPM 1.
[5] Data unavailable for one of the ten agencies.

Technical Note on the Nature of the General Implications of This Case Study and the Limitations to Their Applicability

A CASE STUDY by its very nature can only produce insights that are closer to hypotheses than theories. Applicability of these insights is properly restricted to the class of phenomena studied in the case. Before going on, then, with the implications of this research, first we must define the character of the insights and second draw the boundaries around the area of their applicability.

Scientific research can produce descriptive models, predictive models, or control models. One way to look at these three models is to say that in the descriptive model the researcher identifies independent and dependent variables and creates some order in the system with a catalog and a typology of independent variables. In the predictive model the researcher makes definitive statements about the causal nexus between independent and dependent variables. Since the researcher may not be able to causally relate all the relevant variables, his predictive statements properly take the form: If no Y, than no X. That is, he has isolated an independent variable (Y) without which the dependent variable (X) does not appear. The appearance of Y is a *conditio sine qua non* for the appearance of X. He has identified a necessary, but not a necessary and sufficient, condition. The researcher takes the final step in the control model. He discovers the causal relationships between all the relevant variables in the system, so that he can say: If Y, then X. The independent variable (Y) is a necessary *and* sufficient condition in relation to the dependent variable (X). A control model is also descriptive and predictive; a predictive model is also descriptive. For sure, there are other and more refined ways to look at these models, but the above distinctions permit an adequate characterization of the insights gained in a case study. A case study should produce a descriptive model with a comprehensive and orderly arrangement of the independent and dependent variables in the system. Closely reasoned analysis of the descriptive model can produce some predictive statements of the "if no Y, then no X" type. It is unrealistic to expect a control model with "if Y, then X" statements from a case study, since hypothesis testing is impossible during the observation of nonrepetitive events of a case study. However, from a case study a researcher may distill some "if Y, then X" hypotheses for later testing by scientific methodologies other than case study.

The distinguishing characteristics of the system studied in this research are as follows: Initiative for the symbiotic relationship between change agent and the business organization came from a highly placed executive in the organization who felt a strong and relatively urgent need for change and recognized limitations in the organization's resources for coping with the full scope of the need within the time constraints. In classical terms, the change involved a new marketing orientation achieved through a new planning and control system installed in a newly decentralized organization. This meant a behavioral change at each of the six levels of the organization— each superior would behave differently toward his subordinate and vice versa. At the base of the pyramid, the several hundred organizational units, embracing more than 20,000 people filling the lowest three positions in the hierarchy, were geographically dispersed across the nation and were independent in the work-flow sense. The researcher would like to think that the insights gained in this case study had applicability in situations not fitting the exact description of this client-consultant relationship. He does feel that the insurance industry—and the mutual company in particular—is not so idiosyncratic that what is said here could not apply to other large business organizations dealing with like changes. However, where there is no economic objective function to be maximized (the recent administrative reorganization of the Catholic Church or reorganization of part of the armed forces or a state university system) such different forces are probably at work that these insights would not be readily transferable. Such probably would be true also where the goal orientation centered on attitude or value change. Admittedly, the applicability of these insights in the whole area of managing organizational change must remain an empirical question. Therefore, the researcher intends these implications of his research to extend only to the situations with the limiting characteristics defined above.

Regular Manager Rating Guides

WEEKLY INDIVIDUAL CONFERENCES

1. Does he prepare for the conferences—i.e., know what he wants to get out of them and how he is going to do it?
2. In terms of the time involved, how do his conferences break down between: (a) "Check-in-type" activities (e.g., review of lapses, correspondence, etc.), (b) positive planning (e.g., identifying prospects, planning sales calls, motivating the agent).
3. Over-all when an agent leaves his conference, does he have a better plan for getting business next week than he had when he came in the door? If the answer is "no," his standard of performance on weekly conferences is unsatisfactory.

UNIT CONFERENCES

1. Was the conference properly planned?
   —Logical agenda
   —"Meaty" subjects
   —Opportunity for agent participation
   —Morale building—e. g., use of recognition devices
2. Did it start on time and end as planned?
3. How many men *actively* participated in the conference?
4. How many look bored or anxious to get the conference over with?
5. What *specific* things were said or done that would help the men get more business in the next week?

6. How many of the men went up to the Regular Manager at the end to indicate their interest or satisfaction with the subjects discussed?

FIELD WORK

1. On the average how many hours per week is he in the field with his men working on *sales* activities?
2. Is this field work training, or just selling for the man?
3. On the average how many men does he meet in the field each week?
4. What are his field work plans for the coming week? Are they promising or uninspired?

AGENT MOTIVATION

1. Does he, as an integral part of his weekly conferences, make a definite and positive attempt to motivate his men?
2. At the conclusion of his unit conferences are there any expressions of emotion, enthusiasm, etc.?
3. To what extend do the men in his unit appear to respect and respond to his leadership?
4. How many men confide their personal problems to him?

ORGANIZATION OF TIME

1. Are the weekly conferences scheduled at times that are mutually convenient?
2. How many of his conferences in the past week started on time? Did the unit conference start on time?
3. During the prime selling hours, does he typically get in the field with his men or is he often working in his office?
4. Does he organize his field work in a way that puts him in touch with several of his people each week?

RECRUITING AND SELECTION

1. How many good candidates has he produced in recent months? How much time, if any, does he spend on recruiting? Does he recruit continuously or only when pressed by an open agency position?

2. What recruiting sources and methods does he use? How productive are they? What new methods or sources might he try?

3. How effective are his interviews with prospective candidates? Are his evaluations of candidates sound? Can he sell a candidate on joining the company?

4. Can he administer the Aptitude Test? Does he follow through to make certain that all necessary steps are taken to get the prospective agent started?

Branch Manager Rating Guides

DEVELOPING AND MEETING
SHORT-RANGE GOALS

1. Are his yearly objectives for N.P.M. 2. and manpower growth realistic?
2. Does he meet his yearly objectives? If not, how far off is he?
3. Does he pinpoint the basic problems and improvement opportunities for each of his units?
4. Has he developed sound action plans to maximize improvement in his units and managers?

DEVELOPING AND MEETING
LONG-RANGE GOALS

1. Has his N.P.M. 2. increased in relation to the market potential?
2. Has he expanded (or consolidated) the number of agents in relation to the market potential?
3. Has his turnover of personnel been reduced (or increased)? Why?

DEVELOPING REGULAR
MANAGERS

1. Has he provided leadership, skill training, and/or supervision to make them better managers? What specific time did he spend working with his Regular Managers during the past quarter? What were the results?

2. Has he delegated authority and accountability for end results to his Regular Managers? Has he refrained from making decisions or taking action that should be handled by the Regular Managers?
3. How carefully has he defined the specific shortcomings of each Regular Manager—i.e., along the lines of the six key skills required by Regular Managers?
4. Have the Regular Manager's earnings increased over a period of several years? All things considered, does their rate of development reflect specific help from the Branch Manager—or have they developed solely on their own?
5. Do his Regular Managers confide in him—the bad as well as the good?

CONDUCTING WELL PLANNED, CONSTRUCTIVE, WEEKLY CONFERENCES

1. Does he prepare for the conference—i.e., know what he wants to get out of it and how he will do it?
2. In terms of the total time involved, how do his conferences break down between (a) "check-in" activities, such as past week's results, administrative detail, correspondence, etc., (b) positive planning, such as the Regular Manager's next week's work with his unit, discussion of performance versus objective, etc., (c) counseling activity, such as discussing how to solve certain problems without doing the solving for the Regular Manager, critiqueing his unit meetings, reviewing incidents involving good or bad judgment by the Regular Manager, etc.
3. Over-all, when a Regular Manager leaves the conference, is he a stronger manager than when he came in? Does he know where he excelled or was weak in his past week's activities? Has he solved any problems, or learned how to solve them? Does he have a sound plan and outlook for the week ahead? If the answer to these questions is "no," the Branch Manager's standard of performance is unsatisfactory.

ORGANIZING HIS TIME

1. Does he utilize his time for the greatest gain—i.e., for those units and managers who will respond to his personal attention?

2. In working with units and Regular Managers, does he follow his established priorities?
3. Are his weekly conferences scheduled at times that are mutually convenient? Do they start when scheduled?
4. Does he keep procedural detail minimum through effective administration and delegation of routine matters?

MAINTAINING DISTRICT MORALE

1. Does he keep in touch with the "climate" of the agents—i.e., know the "pulse" of the branch and each man in it? What devices or techniques does he use to do this?
2. Does he hold occasional branch meetings for motivational purposes?
3. Does he outwardly show confidence in his Regular Managers? Does he back them up?
4. Has morale risen or "sagged" under his leadership?

BIBLIOGRAPHY

BOOKS

THE ACTON SOCIETY TRUST. *Management Initiative.* London, 1961.

ALLPORT, GORDON W. *Personality and Social Encounter.* Boston: Beacon Press, 1960.

ARGYRIS, CHRIS. *Interpersonal Competence and Organizational Effectiveness.* Homewood, Ill.: Richard D. Irwin, Inc., and The Dorsey Press, 1962.

————, *et al. Social Science Approaches to Business Behavior.* Homewood, Ill.: Richard D. Irwin, Inc., and The Dorsey Press, 1962.

BENNIS, WARREN G. *Changing Organizations.* New York: McGraw-Hill Book Company, 1966.

————; BENNE, KENNETH D.; AND CHIN, ROBERT. *The Planning of Change.* New York: Holt, Rinehart & Winston, 1962.

————, *et al. International Dynamics.* Homewood, Ill.: Richard D. Irwin, Inc., and The Dorsey Press, 1964.

BLAU, PETER. *The Dynamics of Bureaucracy.* Chicago: University of Chicago Press, 1955.

BURNS, TOM, AND STALKER, G. M. *The Management of Innovation.* Chicago: Quadrangle Books, 1961.

CARTWRIGHT, DARWIN, AND ZANDER, ALVIN. *Group Dynamics.* Evanston, Ill.: Row, Peterson & Co., 1960.

CARZO, ROCCO, AND YANOUZAS, JOHN N. *Formal Organization: A Systems Approach.* Homewood, Ill.: Richard D. Irwin, Inc., and The Dorsey Press, 1967.

CHAPPLE, ELIOT D., AND COON, CARLETON. *Principles of Anthropology.* New York: Holt, Rinehart & Winston, 1942.

————, AND SAYLES, LEONARD R. *The Measure of Management.* New York: The Macmillan Co., 1961.

THE FOUNDATION FOR RESEARCH ON HUMAN BEHAVIOR. *An Action Research for Organization Improvement.* Ann Arbor, Mich., 1960.

————. *Managing Major Change in Organizations.* Ann Arbor, Mich., 1961.

GINZBERG, ELI, AND REILLEY, EWING G. *Effecting Change in Large Organizations.* New York: Columbia University Press, 1957.

GOULDNER, ALVIN W. *Patterns of Industrial Bureaucracy.* New York: The Free Press, 1954.

GUEST, ROBERT H. *Organizational Change: The Effect of Successful Leadership.* Homewood, Ill.: Richard D. Irwin, Inc., and The Dorsey Press, 1962.

HOMANS, GEORGE C. *The Human Group.* New York: Harcourt, Brace & World, 1950.

JUDSON, ARNOLD S. *A Manager's Guide to Making Changes.* London: John Wiley & Sons, Ltd., 1966.

KIRTON, M. J., AND SIDNEY, ELIZABETH. *Case Studies of Management Initiative.* London: Acton Society Trust, 1962.

LAWRENCE, PAUL R. *The Changing of Organizational Behavior Patterns.* Cambridge, Mass.: Harvard University Press, 1958.

LEAVITT, HAROLD J. *Managerial Psychology.* Chicago: University of Chicago Press, 1964.

———— (ed.). *The Social Science of Organizations.* Englewood Cliffs, N.J.: Prentice-Hall, Inc., 1963.

LIPPITT, RONALD; WATSON, JEANNE; AND WESTLEY, BRUCE. *The Dynamics of Planned Change.* New York: Harcourt, Brace & Co., 1958.

MARCH, JAMES G., AND SIMON, HERBERT A. *Organizations.* New York: John Wiley & Sons, Inc., 1959.

MASLOW, ABRAHAM H. *Motivation and Personality.* New York: Harper & Row, 1954.

National Training Laboratory in Group Development. *Explorations in Human Relations: An Assessment of Experience 1947–1953.* Washington, D.C., 1953.

ROGERS, CARL R. *On Becoming a Person.* Cambridge, Mass.: Riverside Press, 1961.

————, AND DYMOND, R. F. *Psychotherapy and Personality Change.* Chicago: University of Chicago Press, 1957.

RONKEN, HARRIET D., AND LAWRENCE, PAUL R. *Administering Changes.* Cambridge, Mass.: Harvard University Press, 1952.

SCHEIN, EDGAR H., AND BENNIS, WARREN G. *Personal and Organizational Change through Group Methods.* New York: John Wiley & Sons, Inc., 1965.

VALIQUET, M. I. "Contribution to the Evaluation of a Management Training Program." Unpublished doctoral dissertation. Massachusetts Institute of Technology, 1964.

WHYTE, WILLIAM FOOTE, AND HAMILTON, EDITH LENTZ. *Action Research for Management.* Homewood, Ill.: Richard D. Irwin, Inc., and The Dorsey Press, 1964.

ARTICLES AND PAPERS

ARENSBERG, CONRAD M. "Behavior and Organization: Industrial Studies," in *Social Psychology at the Crossroads* (eds. JOHN H. ROHRER AND MUZAFER SHERIF). New York: Harper & Row, 1951.

ARGYRIS, CHRIS. "Creating and Evaluating Organizational Change." Paper presented at The Foundation for Research on Human Behavior Conference at the Onchiota Conference Center, Tuxedo, N.Y., July 13, 1965.

BENNE, KENNETH D. "Democratic Ethics and Human Engineering," in *The Planning of Change* (eds. WARREN G. BENNIS, KENNETH D. BENNE, AND ROBERT CHIN). New York: Holt, Rinehart & Winston, 1962.

BENNIS, WARREN G. "Bureaucracy and Social Change: Anatomy of a Failure." Boston: MIT Press, 1963.

———. "A New Role for the Behavioral Sciences: Effecting Organizational Change," *Administrative Science Quarterly* (September, 1963), pp. 126–65.

———. "Theory and Method in Applying Behavioral Science to Planned Organizational Change," *The Journal of Applied Behavioral Science*, I, 4 (October, November, December, 1965), pp. 337–61.

BLAKE, ROBERT R., AND MOUTON, JANE S. "Some Effects of Managerial Grid Seminar Training on Union and Management Attitudes Toward Supervision," *The Journal of Applied Behavioral Science*, II, 4 (October, November, December, 1966), pp. 387–400.

———; BARNES, LOUIS B.; AND GREINER, LARRY E. "Breakthrough in Organization Development," *Harvard Business Review* (November-December, 1964), pp. 133–65.

BUNKER, DOUGLAS R. "Individual Applications of Laboratory Training," *The Journal of Applied Behavioral Science*, I, 2 (April, May, June, 1965), pp. 131–49.

CHAPPLE, ELIOT D. "The Interaction Chronograph: Its Evolution and Present Applications," *Personnel*, Vol. XXV (1949), pp. 295–307.

COCH, LESTER, AND FRENCH, JOHN R. P. "Overcoming Resistance to Change," *Human Relations*, Vol. I, No. 4 (1948), pp. 512–32.

DUBIN, ROBERT. "Business Behavior Behaviorally Viewed," in ARGYRIS *et al., Social Science Approaches to Business Behavior.* Homewood, Ill.: Richard D. Irwin, Inc., and The Dorsey Press, 1962.

GOULDNER, ALVIN W. "Explorations in Applied Social Science—Engineering and Clinical Approaches to Consulting," *Social Problems*, Vol. III, No. 2 (January, 1956), pp. 173–81.

"The Great Boom in Life Insurance Stocks," *Forbes* (April 15, 1964), p. 20 ff.

GREINER, LARRY E., "Patterns of Organization Change," *Harvard Business Review,* 45, 3 (May-June, 1967), pp. 119–30.

————. "Research on the Managerial Grid Approach to Organizational Development." Paper presented at The Foundation for Research on Human Behavior Conference at the Onchiota Conference Center, Tuxedo, N.Y., July 13, 1965.

LEAVITT, HAROLD J. "Applied Organizational Change in Industry: Structural, Technological, and Humanistic Approaches," in *New Perspectives in Organizational Research* (eds. W. W. COOPER, H. J. LEAVITT, AND M. SHELLEY). New York: John Wiley & Sons, 1964.

LEVINE, JACOB, AND BUTLER, JOHN. "Lecture vs. Group Decision in Changing Behavior," *Journal of Applied Psychology,* Vol. 36 (1952), pp. 29–33.

LEWIN, KURT. "Group Decisions and Social Change," in *Readings in Social Psychology* (eds. E. E. MACCOBY, E. L. HARTLEY, AND T. M. NEWCOMB). New York: Henry Holt & Co., 1958.

————. "Studies in Group Decision," in *Group Dynamics: Research and Theory* (eds. D. CARTWRIGHT AND A. ZANDER). Evanston, Ill.: Row, Peterson & Co., 1953.

MANN, FLOYD C. "Studying and Creating Change: A Means to Understanding Social Organization." The Industrial Relations Research Association, No. 17, 1957.

MECHANIC, DAVID. "Some Considerations on the Methodology of Organization Studies," in *The Social Science of Organizations* (ed. HAROLD J. LEAVITT), p. 142. Englewood Cliffs, N.J.: Prentice-Hall, Inc., 1963.

MILES, MATTHEW B. "Changes During and Following Laboratory Training: A Clinical Experimental Study," *The Journal of Applied Behavioral Science,* I, 3 (July, August, September, 1965), pp. 215–42.

————. "Methodological Problems in Evaluating Organization Change: Two Illustrations." Paper presented at The Foundation for Research on Human Behavior Conference at the Onchiota Conference Center, Tuxedo, N.Y., July 13, 1965.

POLLAK, OTTO. "Entrance of the Caseworker into Family Interaction," *Social Casework* (April, 1964).

————. "Issues in Family Diagnosis and Family Therapy," *Journal of Marriage and the Family,* Vol. XXVI, No. 3 (1964), pp. 279–87.

————. "Worker Assignment in Casework with Marriage Partners," *The Social Service Review,* Vol. XXXVII, No. 1 (March, 1963), pp. 41–53.

ROGERS, CARL R. "A Process Conception of Psychotherapy," *The American Psychologist,* Vol. XIII, No. 4 (April, 1958), pp. 142–49.

SAYLES, LEONARD R. "The Change Process in Organizations: An Applied Anthropology Analysis," *Human Organization,* Vol. XXI, No. 2 (Summer, 1962), pp. 62–67.

SCHEIN, EDGAR H. "Management Development as a Process of Influence," *Industrial Management Review,* II, 2 (May, 1961).

SIROTA, DAVID. "An Experiment in Work Measurement." Paper presented at The Foundation for Research on Human Behavior Conference at the Onchiota Conference Center, Tuxedo, N.Y., July 12, 1965.

TANNENBAUM, ROBERT, AND SCHMIDT, WARREN H. "How to Choose a Leadership Pattern," *Harvard Business Review* (March-April, 1958), pp. 95–101.

UROW, HOWARD. "The Reorganization Controversy," *Journal of Industrial Engineering,* Vol. XI, No. 5 (September-October, 1960), pp. 378–82.

WHYTE, WILLIAM F. "Framework for the Analysis of Industrial Relations," *Industrial and Labor Relations Review,* Vol. 3, No. 3 (April, 1950), pp. 393–401.

INDEX

This book has been set in 11 and 10 point Baskerville, leaded 2 points. Chapter numbers are in 12 point News Gothic, and chapter titles are in 18 point News Gothic Condensed. The size of the type page is 27 by 45 picas.